Camping Cookbook

The Outdoor Lover's Complete Guide to Delicious, Healthy, and Nutritious Recipes After a Long Day Outdoors

Trevor Lancaster

Table of Contents

Introduction

Camping is the ultimate way to interact with friend, family and nature. Delaying the daily tough routines and going out with your family for some adventurous experience is not only good for the physical health but also for the mind. As it is said that sound mind has sound body. So, for relaxing the brain and keeping the body active, it is suggested to fill up the ride with the required luggage and find a place nearby your location. That can be any camping site or natural woods.

Camping is of great importance as it can be a way to strength the relationships by spending time with the loved ones. It can be a source of re-connection between the family members as well. It is observed that people usually express much satisfaction and contentment after returning from a camping trip. The feeling of being together gets much stronger when families return from a vacation.

On the other hand, the time spent while camping is a time of learning for the younger ones. The children learn a lot from such experiences. Many practices during a camp trip such as fishing, tenting, fire starting, safety, tying knots, cooking and hiking help them gain acquire a lot of practical skills. It improves their survival skills.

But camping cannot be completed without some deliciously cooked food. Cooking delicious meals on the campfire is not so difficult if one has got the perfectly simple recipes and right ingredients. If one has got some cooking skills, it gets smooth to prepare a yummy meal for all the campers. Some dishes can be half done at home and can be taken to the camping place. There you can finish cooking over the campfire and enjoy it with your family. It is convenient to bring some of the cooking equipment and ingredients with you for easier cooking.

The made ahead recipes helps you to prepare finger licking meals on your camping trip. Freeze dried food can be taken to the camp trip which can e used later to prepare meal. Similarly, you can make use of the freezer bags or ice chest to store your food and use it during your camping trip. There are many options to bake, roast or grill your food depending upon the availability of the equipment. You can take your own skillet or grill to indulge some tasty barbeque or the campfire can be used to toast marshmallows.

All in all, the experience of cooking on a trip with your friends and family is a great way to share love and affection. These are the moments that need to be cherished.

Chapter 1: Camping a healthy practice

"It's much better to camp on a rough day than to work on a pleasant day," any wise guy was sure to claim.

1.1 Background:

Thomas Hiram Holding, who authored the first edition of The Camper's Handbook in 1908, was the father of modern outdoor camping. His desire to camp stemmed from his experiences as a boy: in 1853, with a group of 300, he crossed the prairies of the United States in a train, traveling some 1,200 miles (1,900 km). He camped on a river cruise in the Highlands of Scotland in 1877 and took a return journey the next year. He wrote about these projects in two books.

He later used a bicycle as his vehicle for camping and published Bike and Camp (1898). In 1901, Thomas Hiram Holding founded the world's first camping club, the Cycle Campers Association. By 1907, it had joined with many other clubs to create Great Britain and Ireland Camping Club.

In 1909, Robert Falcon Scott, the renowned Antarctic adventurer, became the Camping Club's first president. All types of camping continue to increase in popularity, from basic to motorized, especially in the USA, Western Europe, and Canada. Most of this trend is the outcome of the increase in recreational vehicle (RV) campsites. In specific, by setting aside asphalt parking areas in the picturesque locations, many commercial and public campsites serve to RVs. In Canada and the USA, where federal and provincial government departments aim to accommodate the increasing public demand, camping on public property is particularly common. Commercial RV campsites typically have power and water connections in an outdoor setting that provides most home comforts.

1.2 Camping: an entertainment venture

Camping is an entertainment venture in which participants engage in temporary outdoor accommodation, usually using tents or constructed or modified shelter vehicles. At one point, for hardy open-air adventurers, camping was only a hard, primitive hobby, but ultimately it became a famous activity for many working-class families.

In camping, the utilization of a tent, campervan, motor home, cottage, a basic structure, or simply no housing may be used at all. As a leisure activity, camping was popular at the beginning of the 20th century. Campers also visit a state or national park, other publicly managed natural areas, and privately-owned campsites. Camping is an integral part of various organizations of young people, such as scouts around the world. It is used to teach teamwork and individuality.

Camping is also an affordable means of accommodation for all those attending large open-air gatherings, including sporting activities and music events. The organizing committee also provides an environment and other essential facilities.

However, camping is highly affected by global uncertainties. With the headlines being circulated, the campers intend to cancel or delay their outings on about the same day. While states are largely revived after shutdowns due to the recent coronavirus and rising domestic tourism, certain people are still not ready for lodging or vacation rental. Plus, moving outside and discovering wide-open areas may sound exceptionally heavenly after spending a lot of time indoors over the past few months. For now, others could still feel more secure living in their tent, where public distancing is far simpler to maintain than at a resort. Around the other corner, there are also camping advantages. You can gain several essential health advantages if you camp regularly:

1.3 Fresh Air

We take most oxygen as we spend lots of time close to several plants. The sensation of satisfaction you get as we take a first big breath at the camping site isn't just in your brain — well, actually, it's, but it's the production of serotonin by extra oxygen. As there's lots of air, the body will operate with minimal pressure. It's not just the biggest benefit in good air. Analysis suggests that outside hours will increase blood pressure, improve metabolism and strengthen the immune system. If you spend a couple of days outdoors, the excess oxygen and reduced toxin levels offer you some important health advantages.

1.4 Socialization

It's usually so much fun to camp on your own, but if you carry a mate or someone from family along, you'll have a great experience, and it will help you maintain a happier, stable friendship. As per reported studies in American Journal for Public Health, social interaction will increase your life and reduce cognitive issues, and, aside from the medical benefits, some close interactions make life more cheerful. Invite your buddies out on the next outing.

1.5 Better moods

Daily hikers will also converse about how they feel good after they get back from a vacation. It is not without pros; spending sufficient time in the sunlight outside the house might also reduce the nervous system's levels of melatonin. Melatonin is that hormone that makes a person feel exhausted and can bring in feelings of despair, so before going on your trip and during your vacation, you can experience greatly improved mood swings because of camping.

1.6 Reduced Tension

Camping helps you a lot to deal with tension and anxiety as well. In just about any way possible, tension will badly affect your health and quality of life, and by providing yourself more stress-free moments at the camping, you exert far less stress on your brain and physical capacities. Lack of tension is correlated with improved higher serotonin levels, the maintained melatonin levels and higher oxygen levels, as mentioned above. It also has a psychological aspect of the task here because when you do anything that you admire, it's not that easy to be offended or upset.

1.7 Physical Exertion

Let us not deny the most witnessed camping value: you spend too much time doing recreational exercises. Even when you're on a fishing adventure, you're burning so many calories than you're trying to burn in the workplace; even if you're on a walk or a bike, you're doing a cardiovascular workout that helps maintain your lungs and heart-healthy. Your extent of physical exertion can differ, but trekkers do burn 100-300 calories/hour. 300-500 calories per hour are consumed by bikers, and fly fishing will burn up to 200 calories an hour. No wonder after a prolonged camping trip, you build up quite an appetite.

1.8 Sunshine

Sunshine on your skin looks wonderful, and there's an evolutionary explanation. You get a lot of Vitamin D while you're out in bright sunshine, which helps the body to accumulate calcium and phosphorus.

Chapter 2: Camping Essentials

Camping is a perfect opportunity to get away with friends and family, or sometimes on your own. You will camp in several city parks, or private camping areas, in the wilderness, and even in your private backyard.

A picnic table, a space to park your car and space to set up your tent are part of several campsites. Most have shared sanitation and water supply as well.

The requirement for so minimal facilities to be outside is part of the fun of camping. But getting a comfortable, easy and homey campsite is also wonderful. It could be best to borrow or hire any of these items if it's your first time camping. You will notice that much of the fun is finding out what to carry along to fulfill your needs when you become a more skilled camper.

Using this helpful camping guide when you're planning to make sure you don't miss something significant. It is a detailed list, and we don't assume you to carry all the stuff along, even though we won't pass judgment if you do. The following are essential items in your camping list of requirements:

2.1 Campsite:

- Sleeping pads

- Sleeping bags

- Table for camp

- Flashlights, headlamps and additional batteries

- Chairs for camp

- Lantern, fuel/batteries mantles and if required

- Tent, stakes and footprint

Optional

- Sunshade, screen house and tarp

- Sleeping bag liners

- Firewood sourced close to the camp area

- Clothesline along with clips

- Hammock

- Cots

- Camp rug

- Tablecloth with clips and tape

2.2 Tools & Repair Items

- Dutch tape

- Multiple tools

- Mattress or pad repairing kit

- Waste bin and small broom

- Axe or saw to cut the firewood

- Sleeve to repair tent-pole

Some additional cords

2.3 Kitchen

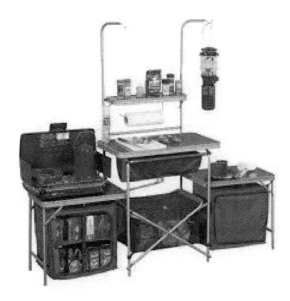

Several campsites have clean drinking water. If you don't, bring your own or be able to handle it if there's a supply of water.

- Potholders and cooking pots

- Utensils for eating

- Fuel and stove

- Cups and mugs

- Matches, fire starters and lighters

- Fry pans

- Knives and spoons

- Bowls and plates

- Can and bottle openers

- Crockery for cooking

- Water bottles

- Coolers

- Sharp knifes

- Towels for washing

- Recycle bags and trash bags

- Sponges and scrubbers

- Cutting boards

- Wash bins and sinks

- Ice substitutes and ice bags

- Soaps (biodegradable)

Optional

- Charcoal

- Griddle

- Camp grill

- Dutch oven

- Ice cream makers

- Grill rack

- Portable tea and coffee maker

- Huge water jugs

- To store kitchen items, larger plastic bags

- Bags, foils and containers for food

- Forks for marshmallow and hot dogs roasting

2.4 Campsite Extras

Most of the following products are optional, but obviously, it depends on how distinct your camp is; navigation resources such as a chart, compass and GPS might be needed.

- **Portable and solar power**

- **reading** material and books

- **Binoculars**

- the night-sky identifier or any Star chart

- Navigation tools

- toys and **games**

- **Pencil /pen** and **Notebook**

- clear plastic bins, **stuff sacks** or **dry bags** to store items

- **Headphones**

- Music player

- **Dog gear**

2.5 Clothing & Footwear

- Socks (wool and synthetic)

- Light-weighted jacket and sleeves

- Sleepwear

- Quick-drying **shorts** and pants

- Moisture-wicking underwear

- **Boots or shoes** suited to the rain

- Shirts with long-sleeve to avoid bugs and sun

- **Moisture-wicking shirts**

2.6 Additional products for cold or rainy weather:

- Warm hats

- Rainwear

- Fleece pants

- Insulated warm vest and jackets

- Mittens and gloves

Optional:

- Bandanas

- Water sandals

- Swimsuits

- Sandals and booties for in the camp

2.7 Health & Hygiene

- Toothbrush and toothpaste

- Towels for quick dry

- Toilet paper

- Prescribed medicine

- Toiletry kit

- Hand sanitizers

- Moisturizer
- First aid box

Protection from bug and sun:

- Lip balm
- Sunglasses
- Insect repellent candles
- Sunscreen
- Sun hat
- Straps for sunglasses

Optional:

- Combs and brushes
- Baby wipes
- Urinary products
- Earplugs
- Cosmetics
- Mirror
- Sanitary towels
- Antiseptic and alcohol wipes
- Eyeglasses
- Contact lenses

Portable showers for camp

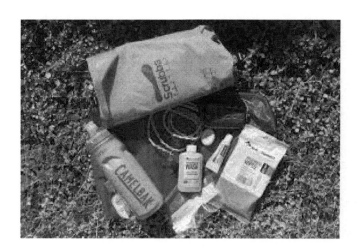

2.8 Camping places

County parks

National Parks provide the best established most costly, most up-to-date campsites. Yet several still provide more primitive solutions accessible on a first-come, first-served basis.

National and Local Parks

State and local parks can be secret jewels, with a handful competing with a national park's magnificence. In a state park, though, it would be quicker to book a reserved spot ahead of time and easiest to have a first-come, first-served site.

Global Forests and BLM Property

The dispersed camp is commonly accessible in national parks and BLM property, all of which may still include several designated campsites. "The basic rule is that you can do camping almost anywhere, and it is not a specified site or specifically mentioned as camping off-limits."

Tribal Property

If you're going to tribal lands, schedule extra time to prepare. Tribes differ widely on what they're offering, where you can find information online and how fast they get back to you.

Private land

Private land is indeed a possibility. Although this could involve knocking on the cottage door and seeking permission to set up a tent, it is most probably a privately owned campground.

Chapter 3: Breakfast recipes

1 Make-Ahead whole grain pancake

Ingredients

- Quick-cooking oats (3 cups)

- Flax seeds (half cup)

- White whole-wheat flour spooned and leveled (3 cups)

- Buckwheat flour spooned and leveled (2 cups)

- All-purpose flour spooned and leveled (2 cups)

- Sugar (1/4 cup)

- Baking soda (1 tbsp.)

- Baking powder (1/4 cup)

- Kosher salt (4 tsp.)

Instructions

1. In a food processor, pulse the oats and flax unless finely chopped, 10 to 15 times.

2. In a container, mix the sugar, oat mixture, baking soda, flours, salt and baking powder.

3. Store in an airtight jar in a refrigerator or freezer for up to 2 months.

2 Many-Seed Toasted Granola

Ingredients

- Old-fashioned rolled oats (6 cups)

- Nuts (such as walnuts, almonds, pistachios), chopped (1 cup)

- Pure maple syrup (1/2 cup)

- Olive, coconut, or sesame oil (1/4 cup)

- Poppy seeds (1/4 cup)

- Sunflower seeds (1/4 cup)

- Sesame seeds (1/4 cup)

- A pure extract of vanilla (2 tsp.)

- Kosher salt (1 tsp.)

- Ground ginger (1/4 tsp.)

Instructions

1. Preheat oven to 350°F. Oil 2 baking sheets gently. In a cup, combine all of the ingredients and, if necessary, ginger.

2. Move to prepared sheets for baking. Bake, stirring once and halfway through revolving pans, until golden brown. Do it for 18 to 24 minutes. Completely cool it.

3 Cheddar, Bacon, and Chive Quick Bread

Ingredients:

- Cooking spray

- All-purpose flour spooned and leveled (1 ½ c.)

- Baking powder (2 tsp.)

- Kosher salt (1/2 tsp.)

- Freshly ground black pepper (1/2 tsp.) plus more for top

- Eggs (2)

- Buttermilk (1/2 c.)

- 4 oz. (1/2 stick) unsalted butter, melted

- 4 oz. sharp Cheddar cheese, grated (1 cup), plus more for top

- 2 oz. Parmesan cheese, grated (1/2 cup)

- Bacon, cooked and crumbled (4 slices)

3 Chopped fresh chives (3 tbsp.)

Instructions:

1. Preheat the oven to 350° F. Oil a 9-by-5-inch loaf pan lightly.

2. In a cup, mix the flour, baking powder, salt, and pepper together. In a measuring cup, mix together the eggs, buttermilk, and butter. To wet to dry ingredients and whisk to mix. Cheddar, parmesan, bacon, and chives folded. Transfer to the packed pan. Sprinkle with some additional pepper and cheddar on top.

3. Bake for 35 to 40 minutes until golden brown and a toothpick inserted in the middle comes out clean. Cool on a wire rack in a pan for 15 minutes. Serve at room temperature or warm.

4 Orange and Pear Muffins

Ingredients

- Baking powder (1 tsp.)

- Orange zest (2 tsp.)

- Apple sauce unsweetened (1/4 cup)

- Granulated sugar (2 tsp.)

- Wheat bran (1 cup)

- Egg (1 large)

- Whole-wheat flour (1 cup)

- Baking soda (1/2 tsp.)

- Ground cinnamon (1/2 tsp.)

- Buttermilk (1/2 cup)

- Olive oil (1/4 cup)

- Kosher salt (1 pinch)

- Red pear (1 medium)

Instructions

1. Heat the oven to 350 degrees F and use ten paper liners to line a 12-hole muffin tray.

2. Combine two teaspoons of sugar and two teaspoons of orange zest in a shallow bowl. Only set aside.

3. Mix the remaining 1/2 cup flour, wheat bran, baking powder, cinnamon, soda, sugar, and salt in a medium dish.

4. Combine the buttermilk, apple sauce, oil, and egg in a wide dish. To the bowl, add the flour mix and blend to incorporate. In the batter, break half the pear into 1/4-inch bits and fold.

5. Between the lined muffin cups, distribute the batter. Cut the remaining pear thinly and place it on the top of the batter.

6. Sprinkle with the orange sugar. Bake for 25 to 30 minutes until a wooden pick inserted in the center comes out clean.

7. For 5 minutes, let the muffins cool in the pan, and then move to a wire rack.

5 Honey Cheerio Nut Turnovers

Ingredients

Turnovers

- Flour, leveled and spooned (1/2 cup)

- Kosher salt (1/2 tsp.)

- Eggs 2 large (divided)

- Sugar (2 tbsp.)

- unsalted butter (1 cup)

- Vegetable shortening (1/4 cup)

- Honey nut cheerios (1 cup)

- Raspberry preserves (1/2 cup)

- Pure almond extract (1/4 tsp.)

- Milk (1 tbsp.)

Sweet Honey Spread

- Confectioners' sugar (1/2 cup)

- Sour cream (1/4 cup)

Instructions

1. In a cup, whisk together the flour, sugar, and salt. Slice the butter and shorten with a pastry cutter or two forks into a flour mixture until it resembles tiny peas.

2. Whisk one egg and 1/4 cup of ice water together.

3. Stir the egg mixture progressively with a fork into the flour mixture; just until the dough starts to shape a ball (add more water if required, one tablespoon at a time).

4. Divide the dough in half; roll it in plastic wrap, push the dough into discs using the wrap. Wrap the plastic around the dough and chill for at least 2 hours and up to 24 hours until it is solid.

5. Roll the dough into 8-by-15-inch rectangles on a finely floured work surface. Slice each into rectangles of 10 (3-by-4-inch).

6. Place rectangles between parchment paper layers; surround with plastic wrap and chill for a minimum of 2 hours and a maximum of 24 hours.

7. Preheat the oven to 425 degrees'. Cover the parchment with two baking sheets. In a pot, stir the preserves and almond extract together. Beat the remaining egg in a mixing bowl with the sugar.

8. Functioning with one dough rectangle at a time, top with preserves mixture, one tablespoon, spreading nearly to the margins.

9. Brush the sides with raw eggs. Cover it with a new piece of dough and press the sides to seal

using a fork.

10. Put on baking sheets that have been prepared. With the remaining dough, the mixture, and the egg was repeat steps. Brush the egg wash on the pies; chill for 20 minutes.

Make honey spread

1. Whisk together the candy sugar, sour cream, pure honey, and a sprinkle kosher salt in a small bowl until blended. The honey spread is ready.

2. Bake, turning once the pans until golden brown, 18 to 22 minutes. To cool absolutely, move turnovers to wire racks.

3. Use Sweet Honey Paste to spread surfaces and dust with sprinkles and Honey Nut Cheerios

6 Make-Ahead Easy Parfaits

Ingredients

- Blueberries (1 cup)

- Water (1/4 cup)

- Heavy cream (1 cup)

- Fresh lemon juice (1 tbsp.)

- Strawberries (2 cups)

- Canning jars (8)

- Sugar (1/4 cup)

- Angel food cake (10 oz.)

- Shredded coconut (1/2 cup)

Instructions

1. Stir the sugar and water together in a 1-quart saucepan. Heat to a full boil, stirring occasionally; stir in the lemon juice and the blueberries.

2. Pull back from the heat. Enable it to cool properly.

3. Whip the cream in a wide bowl with a medium-speed mixer until soft peaks appear. Fold softly

in the mixture of cooled blueberries.

4. On the bottom of 1 canned jar, put a single layer of angel food cake. Put two teaspoons of straw-berries, then two tablespoons of whipped blueberry cream on top.

5. Repeat the layering of the cake, whipped cream and strawberries. Repeat with seven jars left.

6. Serve instantly or cover the screw caps and chill in the fridge for up to 1 day. Top each parfait with one tablespoon coconut before serving.

7 Jelly Muffins with Peanut Butter

Ingredients

- Wheat bran (1 cup)

- Buttermilk (1/2 cup)

- Creamy Peanut Butter (10 tsp.)

- Granulated sugar (1/2 cup)

- Baking soda (1/2 tsp.)

- Ground cinnamon (1/2 tsp.)

- Water (1 tbsp.)

- Unsweetened applesauce (1/4 cup)

- Olive oil (1/4 cup)

- Large Egg (1)

- Baking powder (1 tsp.)

- Small red grapes (1 cup)

- Whole-wheat flour (1 cup)

- Seedless jam (1/4 cup)

- Kosher salt (1 pinch)

Instructions

1. Heat the oven to 350 degrees F and use ten paper liners to line a 12-hole muffin tray.

2. Combine the flour, sugar, baking powder, soda, wheat bran, cinnamon, and salt in a medium dish.

3. Mix the apple sauce, oil, buttermilk, and egg in a wide bowl. To the container, add the flour mix and blend to incorporate.

4. Fold the grapes in. Distribute half of the batter between the lined muffin cups.

5. Cover with one teaspoon of peanut butter each, and then add the remainder of the batter. Bake for 25 to 27 minutes, until a wooden pick placed in the middle, comes out neat.

6. For 5 minutes, let the muffins cool in the pan, and then move to a wire rack.

7. Meanwhile, mix the jam with one tablespoon of water in a shallow bowl.

8. Glaze some jam mixture on the muffins only before eating.

8 Campfire pineapple and hot ham sandwiches

Ingredients

- Cheddar cheese (6 slices)

- Deli sliced ham (9 oz)

- Dijon mustard (2 Tbsp)

- pineapple rings (6), if desired, cut in half

- French Rolls Rhodes Artisan (6), soften to normal room temperature

- Honey (1 Tbsp)

Instructions:

1. Split half of the rolls. Mix the Dijon mustard with the honey and spread with the honey mixture on each roll's bottom.

2. Assemble each sandwich like this: Place a couple of bits of ham on the honey-mustard.

3. Cover the ham with a ring of pineapple, sliced in half if you like. Cover the pineapple with a cheddar cheese slice and roll the top half.

4. Cover each sandwich well with high duty aluminum foil. Place the sandwiches over hot coals or a grill rack until hot, depending on the fire temperature, for around 20 minutes.

5. Alternatively, you should bake these sandwiches in 400 degrees Fahrenheit oven for 15 minutes right above the wire rack. Unwrap gently and eat!

9 Cinnamon roll-ups for campfire

Ingredients

1. ·Crescent rolls (1 package)

2. Cinnamon (1 tbsp)

3. Sugar (1/4 cup)

Instructions:

1. in a wide bowl, mix sugar and cinnamon

2. Segregate the crescent rolls and fold it around the skewer.

3. Roll it in a combination of cinnamon sugar

4. Cook over the campfire for five minutes, turning often.

5. Optional-Mix 1/4 cup of icing sugar and 2-3 tablespoons of water together to form a glaze and a drizzle over cooked rolls

10 Breakfast Burritos for Camping

Ingredients

- Old El Paso flour tortillas (8) (12-inch)

- olive oil (1/2 tsp)

- Old El Paso Taco Seasoning (1 tsp)

- Chopped cilantro (1/4 cup)

- Frozen hash browns (1 cup)

- Cooked ham, diced (8 oz)

- Eggs (12)

- Can of **Chilies** (1 (4.5 oz)

- shredded 8 oz of cheddar cheese (2 cups)

Instructions

1. In a large skillet, warm the olive oil. Add the hash browns and cook over medium heat for a minute, stirring continuously. Add ham to it.

2. Continue to cook around 8-10 minutes, until the hash browns and ham both have golden brown, stirring regularly,

3. Meanwhile, beat the eggs gently in a large bowl. Mix the taco seasoning. Once the hash browns and the ham are golden, add the eggs onto the skillet.

4. Cook; constantly stir until the eggs are ready.

5. Stir in the cilantro, cheese and green chilies.

6. Heat the tortillas.

7. Add 1/8 of the egg mix in the middle of each tortilla. Roll up and roll firmly in foil, much like a burrito.

8. Keep it in a refrigerator or a zip lock bag.

9. Put wrapped burritos in burning coals by the flames when to be cooked.

10. Let the burritos remain in the coal, rotating once, around 10-15 minutes until cooked through. (The time depends on how warm the fire is)

11 Swiss croissants with hot ham

Ingredients

- Dijon mustard (2 tsp)

- Honey (1tsp)

- Brown sugar (1 tsp)

- Croissants split (4)

- Swiss cheese (8 slices)

Instructions:

1. Mix the mustard, brown sugar and honey

2. Spread the mustard honey mix on either side of the four cut croissants.

3. Put a piece of Swiss on each part of the croissants.

4. Cover the lower half of each croissant with as much ham as you want.

5. Put these two halves back together.

6. Cover it in foil.

7. Put in the refrigerator for now or later

8. Put in 350 preheated ovens for 10-15 minutes. Delicious!

12 Pumpkin French toast

Ingredients

- Whole milk (⅔ cup)

- Pumpkin spice (2 tsp)

- Four large eggs

- Sea salt (½ tsp)

- Butter (3 tsp)

- Pumpkin puree (½ cup)

- Thick cut bread (12 slices), such as brioche or texas toast

- Sugar (2 tsp)

Instructions

1. Beat the eggs in a big enough bowl first to fit a slice of the toast.

2. Mix the milk, pumpkin's purée, the sugar, the pumpkin's spice, and the salt until well combined.

3. In a pan, melt a tablespoon of butter over medium heat.

4. Dip the bread in the batter and let it sink for around 10 seconds on either side.

5. Let the extra drip off, then put in the skillet and fried until golden and crispy on each hand, around 3 minutes on each side.

6. Repeat with the rest of the bread and add more butter to the pan as needed.

7. Serve with maple syrup, pumpkin butter (optional) and a nice cup of coffee. Have fun

13 Stove Chilaquiles

Ingredients

- Vegetable oil (1/3 cup)

- One Can of el pato sauce (7oz) (or a chopped jalapeño and 1 cup tomato sauce)

- Cloves of garlic (2), minced

- 2 – 4 large eggs

- Corn tortillas (6), sliced into wedges

- Red onion (half), diced

- Half tsp salt

Instructions

1. Heat the oil in a saucepan over hot temperature.

2. Once the oil is warmed, place the tortilla triangles in a single layer and fry until golden brown for another few minutes.

3. Remove and put aside to drain on a paper towel. Repeat the remaining of the tortillas.

4. Lower to medium flame. Add the red onions to the residual oil and cook and stir for a few minutes once they tend to soften.

5. Add the garlic and continue cooking for around 30 seconds, then add the tomato paste, salt, and water to the pan.

6. Bring to a boil, and then incorporate some fried tortillas. Mix to coat.

7. To prepare the eggs, transfer the tortillas to either the skillet's outer edges to form a well in

the middle.

8. Dump the eggs in the sauce and prepare to your taste – you may scramble them or cover the mixture and allow them to poach in the gravy quickly.

9. End up serving mostly with toppings of everyone's preference. Enjoy it!

14 Breakfast tacos

Ingredients:

- Yellow onion (1 small)

- 4-6 large eggs*

- Bell pepper (1 large)

- For coating the pan, butter, ghee, or avocado oil

- Tortillas (4 small)

- Shredded cheddar cheese (1 cup) (or you can use a block of cheese sliced into some pieces per taco)

- Pepper and salt to taste

- One jalapeno (optional)

Instructions

1. Cut into small slices of bell pepper and onion.

2. On your camp stove, place a cast-iron pan over moderate heat.

3. To the pan, add 1 Tablespoon of clarified butter and afterward, add the onions and bell pepper strips.

4. Cook for around 5 minutes, stirring often.

5. If using the jalapeno, cut it and incorporate it into the skillet with both the peppers and onions.

6. Cook until the onion becomes transparent in 3-5 more minutes.

7. Scramble the eggs into a different bowl while the bell peppers and onions simmer. Put the prepared peppers and onions in a large bowl with a pinch of salt and pepper.

8. Add a little more ghee to the cast iron pan and then place the scrambled eggs. Prep the eggs.

9. Cut the cheese with all of the other toppings you need when the eggs are getting prepared.

10. Place them in a large bowl when the eggs are ready and heat the tortillas in a hot pan.

11. Place the tacos together! Place on your favorite cheese, pepper, eggs, and onions. Serve instantly.

15 Vanilla almond berry oatmeal

Ingredients:

- freeze-dried blueberries (1/4 cup)

- freeze-dried strawberries (1/4 cup)

- sliced almonds (1/4 cup)

- **RX Vanilla Almond Nut Butter** (1 packet)

- instant oats (1/2 cup)

Instructions:

At home:

1. Place the oats, cold-dried strawberries, sliced almonds, and freeze-dried blueberries into a medium lidded container.

2. Placed the almond butter package in the jar. Should not open the almond butter package yet. Wait till you're at the campsite.

3. Seal the bag properly and double bag it if required. You don't want the bag to tear.

At Camp:

1. Open a bag and pull out the almond butter package.

2. Pour the oat blend into your medium bowl and add almost about 1 cup of hot water.

3. Ultimately, open the almond butter bag and stir it in.

16 Bacon and pepper breakfast quesadillas

Ingredients

- Bacon slices (4)

- Shallot (1)

- Green bell pepper (1)

- Cooking oil or butter

- Four large eggs

- Flour tortillas (2)

- Cheddar cheese

Instructions

1. Cook the bacon over a moderate flame in a cast-iron skillet.

2. After frying, take out from the pan and place it all on a plate, lined with towers of paper.

3. Slice the shallots and pepper, apply the bacon fat to the pan. Fry for two or three minutes.

4. Put the eggs in the skillet with the peppers and shallots. Using a fork or a wooden spoon, to scramble it in the skillet while it heats. Remove from the heat and reserve until the eggs have been fully prepared.

5. Cut the bacon into small pieces and add to the eggs.

6. In the cast iron skillet, put a tortilla over a moderate flame, and cover with cheese slices the half of the tortilla.

7. Place half of the eggs with the combination of bacon. Top off with some extra cheese.

8. Fold the tortilla halfway and cook on either side for roughly 2 minutes before the cheese melted.

9. Cut to serve the quesadilla right away. Repeat with the leftover mixture of eggs and the second tortilla.

17 Strawberry chocolate hazelnut s'mores

Ingredients:

- Freeze-dried strawberries (1 pack)

- Marshmallows (4)

- Graham crackers (1 pack)

- Chocolate hazelnut spread (1 jar) for example, nutella

Instruction

1. Apply a coating of chocolate hazelnut spread over half of each graham cracker.

2. Put some slices of frozen strawberries on one of the graham crackers above the chocolate.

3. Slowly toast the marshmallow over the campfire until it gets puffy and golden colored.

4. Place the toasted marshmallow on top of the frozen strawberries and use the upper half of the graham cracker to slip the marshmallow off the stick. Enjoy it!

18 Pear and Orange Muffins

Ingredients

- Large egg (1)

- Granulated sugar (2 tsp.)

- Granulated sugar (1/2 cup)

- Wheat bran (1 cup)

- Red pear (1 medium)

- Orange zest (2 tsp.)

- Whole-wheat flour (1 cup)

- Baking soda (1/2 tsp.)

- Ground cinnamon (1/2 tsp.)

- Baking powder (1 tsp.)

- Kosher salt (1 pinch)

- Buttermilk (1/2 cup)

- Unsweetened applesauce (1/4 cup)

- Olive oil (1/4 cup)

Instructions

1. Preheat oven to 350 ° F and cover a 12-hole muffin pan with ten liners of paper. In a shallow bowl, mix 2 tsp of sugar with 2 tsp of orange zest. Set it back.

2. In a wide bowl, add the rest of the half cup of sugar, flour, wheat bran, baking powder, cinnamon, soda and salt.

3. Combine the buttermilk, apple sauce, oil and egg in a wide bowl. Transfer the flour mix to a dish and blend.

4. Slice half the pear to 1/4-inch parts and put it in the batter. Divide the mixture between the lined muffin cups.

5. Cut the remainder pear finely and place it on top of the batter. Sprinkle with orange sugar and cook until the wooden pick injected directly in the center comes out clear, for 25 to 30 minutes.

6. Allow the muffins to chill in the pan for 5 minutes and then move to the serving plate.

19 Campfire Skillet Oreo Cinnamon Buns

Ingredients

- Cream cheese (4 ounces)

- Oreo Cookies (6 crushed)

- Cinnamon bun dough (1 tube of pre-made)

- White sugar (1 tablespoon)

- Baking sheet or skillet

Instructions

1. Mix the cream cheese, Oreos and sugar.

2. Take out the cinnamon buns from the jar and unroll them.

3. Into the inside of each unrolled cinnamon bun, spread the cream cheese mixture and roll them back together.

4. Put in a pan.

5. Heat in the BBQ or cover in tinfoil and prepare on your fireplace until lightly browned and cooked.

6. When cooled a little, remove and place any remaining cream cheese mixture evenly on top. Relax! Enjoy!

20 Hill-Man Casserole Breakfast

Ingredients

- Pork sausage (1 pound)

- Eggs (1 dozen), whisked

- Simply Potatoes (2 packages), diced or hash browns

- Medium onion (1) has to be chopped

- Sliced cheddar cheese (1 cup)

- Pepper and salt to taste

Instructions

1. Cook the sausage inside a cast-iron Dutch oven over a heated coal pit. Pick and dry the sausage on paper towels.

2. Sauté the onion in the leftover cooking liquid until soft. Include the potatoes and cook until tender and slightly browned. Layer the potatoes uniformly on the bottom and top with cheese, eggs and sausage. Put the cover on top and place 16 burning coals on the lid.

3. Bake for 25 minutes until the eggs are ready. End up serving!

21 Camping Chicken Kabobs with Maple Siracha

Ingredients

- Siracha sauce (1 tbsp)

- soy sauce (1/4 cup)

- medium pineapple (1cubed)

- maple syrup (1/4 cup)

- red bell pepper (1cubed)

- chicken breasts (2 large cubed)

Instructions

1. In a huge re-sealable plastic container, position the sliced chicken breasts.

2. 2 Toss the maple syrup, soy sauce, and sriracha sauce together.

3. Pour it over the chicken surface and rub it into the chicken.

4. Marinate in an icebox for a minimum of 15 minutes to 24hrs.

5. Soak your wood skewers in water for about 10 minutes until the chicken is marinated.

6. Then skewer each chicken bits, pineapple and red bell pepper directly onto the skewer.

7. Barbecue the chicken until fully cooked. Approximately ten minutes.

8. Eat and relax!

22 Camping oven Dumplings and Dutch Chicken

Ingredients

- 1 broiler chicken (1), shredded or chunked (2 to 3 pounds)

- Minced fresh parsley (1 tablespoon)

- Chopped onion (1 cup)

- Celery ribs (4), sliced

- Water (3 cups)

- medium carrots (3), sliced

- Celery seed (1 teaspoon)

- Salt (1 teaspoon)

- Black pepper (1/4 teaspoon)

- Rubbed sage (2 teaspoons), divided

- Baking mix/ biscuit (3 cups)

- Milk (3/4 cup)

Instructions

1. Put the water and chicken in a Dutch oven. Cover it and let it go to a boil.

2. Lower the heat to slow cook; simmer for around 30 minutes, until the chicken is juicy.

3. Take the chicken out of the kettle, bone it and cube.

4. Take the cabbage, celery, onions, celery seed, one teaspoon of sage, salt and pepper and the chicken, and add all these back to the kettle.

5. Just get these to the boiling.

6. Lower the flame

7. For 45-60 min, cover and simmer until the vegetables are soft.

8. Mix the biscuit blend, parsley, milk, and leftover sage to shape a hard mixture for dumplings or just use the can of biscuits.

9. Drop the tablespoonfuls into the chicken mix that is simmering.

10. 10 Cap for 15 min and cook.

11. Instantly serve.

23 Campfire Mac n Cheese

Ingredients

- 12-16 ounces kielbasa (1 package), 1-inch rounds slices

- Milk (1/4-1/2 cup)

- jarred Alfredo sauce (8-10 oz)

- dry elbow macaroni noodles (1/2 cups)

- Blend cheddar and mozzarella (1/2 cup)

- Pepper and salt to taste

Instructions

1. Cook the kielbasa in a wide cast iron pan or dutch oven. Drain all the extra fat and keep aside

2. Cook the pasta according to product instructions in a separate pan. Drain and wash with cool water. You can make noodles at home as well. To prevent the cooking process, stun them with ice water and store them in either a sealed bag in the refrigerator.

3. To make a sauce, add Alfredo sauce, noodles, cheese and start adding milk (begin with 1/4 of a bowl and add more of it if required). For good taste, season it with pepper and salt

4. Heat for 5-10 mins on a grater above coals, frequently stirring until the cheese is completely melted.

5. Pull from the flames and serve instantly

24 Camping peasant's breakfast

Ingredients

- Large **potatoes** (4)

- Sliced **bacon**

- Medium **onion** (3), diced

- Large **eggs** (4)

- Pepper and salt to taste

- Unsweetened **butter**

- Some **parsley** (for garnish)

Instructions

1. Cook the potatoes in hot, salted water with the skins until cooked.

2. Cool, remove the skin or keep skins on, slice or cube

3. Slice bacon into small strips and cook to the appropriate crispness on moderate heat. Pat dry o on a paper towel.

4. Includes approx. Two tablespoons of butter in the bacon oil and cook the onions until they are translucent.

5. Put the potatoes in the onion pan and fry until the crust is formed. Return your bacon.

6. Put the eggs into the potatoes and do everything to properly scramble them around. For good taste, add salt and pepper.

7. Be cautious with the salt, as the bacon is already salty. Garnish it with parsley.

8. Nice as a side dish, brunch, of instance, or as a main course of 2 with just a green salad.

9. The cooking period is after the cooling of the potatoes.

26 Shakshuka

Ingredients:

- Seeded & sliced red bell pepper 1

- Olive oil 1 tbsp

- Sliced & seeded poblano peppers 1

- Chopped garlic 3 cloves

- Paprika 2 tsp

- Diced small onion 1

- Cumin 1 tsp

- Minced parsley

- Diced tomatoes 14 oz cup

- Feta cheese 1/4 cup

- Pepper & salt

Instructions:

1. In your pan, hot oil over med heat. Swirl to cover when the poblano, onions & red bell peppers are warmed, cook for five mins or the color shifts to brown, stirring if possible. Then cook the paprika, garlic & cumin for around thirty seconds until it is fragrant.

2. Placed all the tomatoes and their juices. Turn the heat down & boil for ten minutes to allow the mixture to thicken.

3. Split the eggs into the sauce, spreading them evenly apart. Till the whites are set, cover & let all the eggs boil, 5 to 7 mins. You could spoon the sauce on top, as needed, to enable them to cook fully.

4. Serve with sliced parsley, feta cheese, and a few crusty bread pieces.

Chapter 4: Lunch Recipes

1. Hot Dogs with Quick Beans

Ingredients

- For grill skillet, use canola oil.

- Onion, diced (1 small)

- Olive oil (1 tbsp.)

- A medium can of white beans, washed, (1)

- Plum tomatoes, finely chopped, (4)

- Molasses (2 tbsp.)

- Garlic, finely chopped, (2 cloves)

- Black pepper finely grounded and kosher salt.

- Hot dog buns (6)

- Worcestershire sauce (2 tsp.)

- Red wine vinegar (2 tsp.)

- hot dogs (6)

- Mustard, relish, and ketchup for serving

Instructions

1. Arranged a grill to cook directly and indirectly, and warm to medium. Once it is warm, cleaned and lightly oiled is grate it with canola oil.

2. Heat the olive oil in either a 9-inch cast-iron pan over high heat. Add the onion and braise, often stirring, until golden, for 2 to 4 mins.

3. Add the beans, garlic, tomatoes, and molasses. Use pepper and salt as per taste. Transfer your skillet to low flame. Cook and often stirring, until tomatoes are softened, for 15 minutes. Take away from the stove. Add vinegar and Worcestershire.

4. Cook hot dogs over medium heat, turning regularly, until softened through for 5 to 6 mins. Grill the buns, if you like.

5. End up serving hot dogs in buns along with bean, mustard, ketchup, and relish on the side.

2 Chicken Nachos with Black Bean

Ingredients

- Rotisserie shredded chicken (3 1/2 cup)

- Small chopped onion (half)

- red enchilada sauce (1 cup)

- freshly obtained corn kernels (1 cup)

- pepper-Jack cheese, 12 ounces, divided ((around 3 cups)

- canned black beans, washed, (1)

- freshly black pepper and Kosher salt

- tortilla chips (8 ounces)

- Fresh lime wedges and cilantro for garnish

Instructions

1. Arrange the indirect cooking grill and heat to low. In a pan, mix the chicken, onion, enchilada sauce, beans, maize, and 8 ounces of cheese. With salt and pepper, season.

2. Tear the aluminum foil into six 12-inch squares. , On one end of a piece of foil, put one-sixth of the chicken mixture, chips, and the remaining cheese, leaving the 3-inch border.

3. To build a package and crimp edges to secure, fold the foil over the filling. Repeat with the leftover foil, chips, cheese and chicken mixture.

4. Grill packets until cheese are melted, and chicken is cooked through, 6 to 10 mins, over low heat.

5. Move packets to dishes and open them with care. garnish with cilantro and serve with wedges of lime

3 Beer-Steamed Chicken

Ingredients

- Garlic cloves, finely chopped (3)

- Hot sauce (such as Cholula) (1 tbsp.)

- Dijon mustard (2 tsp.)

- Grounded cumin (1 tsp.)

- 2 tsp. Chili powder

- Black pepper, freshly ground.

- Kosher salt to taste

- Chicken boneless, skinless thighs (4 lb.)

- A 12-ounce bottle of dark Mexican beer (1)

- Canola oil, divided into batches (2 tbsp.)

- Sauce from chipotles can (3 tbsp.)

- Jalapeño, corn tortillas, ranch coleslaw, chopped radishes, diced pickled jalapenos, cilantro, lime wedges and sliced carrots for serving

Instructions

1. In a zip-top container, combine the adobo sauce, spicy sauce, garlic, mustard, chili powder, cumin and one teaspoon of salt and pepper.

2. Include the chicken, close the container, and then switch the coat over. Refrigerate for at least 4 hours or a maximum of 12 hours.

3. Preheat the oven to 350 degrees.

4. Heat 1 tablespoon of oil over medium to high flame in a big Dutch oven.

5. Roast chicken in batches, 3 to 4 mins per side, until browned (adding more oil if required), take out batches on a plate.

6. Put all the chicken back in the Dutch oven and gradually add some beer. Simmer for 4 to 6 mins until it has been gradually reduced.

7. Cap and bake for 40 to 45 mins, until the chicken is juicy. With two forks, remove the chicken and shred the flesh.

8. Bring to a boil the cooking liquid for 4 to 6 mins over a moderate flame until slightly emulsified. Put the chicken and turn to coat. With salt and pepper, season.

9. Serve alongside jalapeño, tortillas, Ranch Coleslaw, sliced radishes, jalapeños, cilantro, onions, and lime wedges.

4 Parched Sausage with Pink Lady Apples and Cabbage

Ingredients

- Sweet Italian sausage links (6 small/medium)

- Fresh apple cider (1 cup)

- Olive oil (1 tbsp.)

- Pink Lady apples, sliced (2)

- Red cabbage, cut into slices half inch-thickness

- Red onion, finely sliced (1/2)

- Kosher salt and black pepper freshly crushed.

- Freshly obtained cider vinegar (2 tbsp.)

Instructions

1. Heat oil in a broadcast iron pan over medium heat. Include the sausage and fry, turning regularly, until golden brown, for 6 to 8 mins; move to a tray.

2. Reduce heat to mild and add apples, slice the side down. Spread the onion and the cabbage around the apples.

3. Season to taste, with pepper and salt. Sauté, stirring onions regularly, until apples are lightly browned, for 4 - 5 minutes.

4. Toss apples. Return the sausage to the pan, nestling among all the vegetables. Add the vinegar and cider.

5. Simmer, move and turn the sausages frequently until the sausages have cooked completely, and the apples are soft for 18 to 20 mins.

5 Prime grilled burger

Ingredients

- 60/40 ground beef (1 1/2 lb.)

- Dried fresh spices, only for seasoning

- Freshly ground black pepper and kosher salt

- Canola oil, for grill grates or pan

Instructions

1. Separate ground beef into four 6-ounce parts, form roughly into patties almost as large as the buns you're utilizing, and about 1/2-inch thickness.

2. Create a slight concave indentation in the center of each patty. It is going to support the burger from doming as they fry.

3. Salt patties on either side (add at least 1/2 teaspoon of salt per patty). Season to perfection with spices and pepper

4. Arranged a grill for active cooking and heat to moderate or heat a cast iron pan on top of the stove over moderate flame.

5. When heated, gently brush the grill or oil the pan. Note: The oil is going to smoke. While cooking indoors, we suggest switching on your exhaust fan and opening the windows.

6. Grill or sauté burgers around 3 and 5 mins per side.

7. Test the ideal flavor and texture with an automatic meat thermometer embedded in the edge of the burger.

8. Cook to 120°F for rarely cooked burgers. For the medium-rare: 130°F. For the medium: 140°F.

9. For the medium well: 150°F. Cook to 160°F to guarantee that the burger is well cooked. Do not cook above 160°F, or the burger would dry up.

6 Marinated Chicken and Onion Kebabs

Ingredients

- Plain yogurt (1/2 cup)

- Grated fresh ginger (1 tbsp.)

- Garlic cloves, minced (2)

- Garam masala (1 tsp.)

- Lemon zest (2 tsp.)

- Lemon juice (2 tsp.)

- Grounded turmeric (1 tsp.)

- Fresh grounded black pepper and Kosher salt

- Canola oil, for grilling

- Boneless chicken, cut into 11/2-inch parts (1 1/2 lb.)

- Flatbread or naan (4 pieces)

- Medium-size red onion, cut into 1-inch wedges (1)

- Cilantro and Cucumber Yogurt Sauce

Instructions

1. In a bowl, mix yogurt, ginger, garlic, garam masala, lemon zest, turmeric and juice, and 1/2 tsp of each pepper and salt. Include the chicken and mix until combined. Allow marinating for fifteen minutes.

2. Set grill to low heat. When the grill is heated, clean and lightly oiled, thread the chicken and onion over six large skewers.

3. Grill, stirring regularly, until the chicken is cooked completely and the onion is soft, ten to fifteen minutes.

4. Grill flatbread till evenly browned, around 1 minute on each side.

5. Serve the kebabs and the flatbread with the Cucumber and Parsley yogurt sauce on the side.

7 Grilled fixin's hot dogs

Ingredients

To prepare grilled hot dogs

- hot dogs (8)

- Hot dog buns (1 pack)

- Black pepper taste

- Onion fixin' and zesty pickle

- Pickles neatly chopped (4)

- Freshly diced white onion (1/4)

- Fresh flat-leaf parsley (3 tbsp.)

- Whole-grain mustard (2 tbsp.)

- Kosher salt to taste

Tangy horseradish fixin'

- Black pepper

- White wine vinegar (1 tbsp.)

- Prepared horseradish (3 tbsp.)

- Sour cream (2 tbsp.)

- finely chopped purple cabbage (1/4)

- Mayonnaise (1 tbsp.)

- Sugar (1 tsp.)

- finely chopped scallion (1)

- grated large carrot (1)

- Fresh dill chopped (2 tbsp.)

- Kosher salt

Spicy chiles fixin'

- White wine vinegar (1 cup)

- Coriander seeds (1 tsp.)

- Sugar (2 tbsp.)

- Kosher salt (1/4 tsp.)

- Finely diced small red onion (1)

- Finely chopped Fresno chilies (2)

Instructions

1. Grill 8 hot dogs on a moderate fire, turning regularly, until finely charred and cooked, for 4 to 5 minutes.

2. Grill the buns until nicely browned, if needed. Serve for any almost all of the following fixins.

3. Create Lemony Pickle and Onion Fixin': add pickles, white onion, fresh parsley and whole-grain mustard in a dish. Season to taste, with pepper and kosher salt. Prepare about 2 cups.

Making Tangy Horseradish Fixin'

1. stir together the cooked horseradish (pressed of excess moisture), the white wine vinegar, the sour cream, the mayonnaise and the sugar in a dish.

2. Include any purple cabbage (about 2 cups), carrots, scallion and fresh dill. Season to taste, with organic pepper and salt.

3. Let it settle down, frequently turning, for 15 minutes. Prepare two cups

4. Prepare Hot Chiles Fixin': put white wine vinegar, sugar, coriander seeds and kosher salt to a boil in a deep pot over medium flame.

5. Turn off the heat and include chili peppers and the red onion.

6. Allow to sit, frequently toss, for a minimum of 25 minutes or up to three days. Make around 1 1/2 cups.

8 The Campfire Cocktail

Ingredients

- Liquid smoke (2 - 3 drops)

- Whiskey (1 1/2 oz)

- Ginger simple syrup (1oz)

- Lemon juice (1tsp.)

- A squeeze of honey (as per taste)

- Ginger+ Lemon peel for serving.

For the simple Ginger syrup

- Equal portions of sugar and water

- Fresh cut ginger

Instructions:

1. Firstly, clean the glass with a few drops of liquid smoke. Make sure to get the extra liquid smoke off your glass; you will have to clear it a few times.

2. Add the ice to the cocktail shaker and garnish with the bourbon, the simple syrup, the lemon juice and the sugar.

3. Give it a shake for 12-15 seconds. The shaker is meant to be cool and frosty.

4. Put liquid in the liquid smoke glass; garnish with the ice.

5. Torch the lemon peel and rub it across the glass surface; drop that in. Add the ginger pieces (you should use the simple syrup ginger).

To prepare simple syrup

6. Mix the sugar and water and dissolve on moderate flame; gently stir.

7. When the sugar is dissolved, withdraw from the fire and add in the ginger pieces. Please allow it to be steep.

8. Add in the plastic bottle and store it in the fridge.

9 Shrimp scampi foil packets

Ingredients:

- Medium shrimp, skinned and deveined (1 1 /2)

- Dry white wine (2 tsp.)

- Melted, unsalted butter (1/2 cup)

- Garlic cloves, minced (4)

- Freshly chopped thyme leaves (1 tsp.)

- Freshly chopped rosemary (1 tsp.)

- Freshly chopped parsley (2 tsp.)

- Fresh lemon juice, to taste (1 tsp.)

- Crushed red pepper flakes (1/2 tsp.)

- Lemon zest (1)

- Fresh black pepper and Kosher salt, to taste

Instructions:

1. Preheat the gas or charcoal bbq over high temperatures.

2. In a wide bowl, mix shrimp, garlic, butter, wine, thyme, rosemary, lemon juice, red pepper flakes and lemon zest; season to taste with pepper and salt.

3. Split four sheets of the foil, around 12-inch in length.

4. Distribute the shrimp mix into four equal parts and add in the middle of each foil in the single sheet

5. Fold each foil packet's four sides over all of the shrimp, tightly covering and securing the packets tightly.

6. Put the foil packets on the flame and cook for around 10-12 mins until cooked completely.

7. Serve instantly; if required, garnish with parsley.

10 Campfire perfect nachos

Ingredients

- Ground beef (1 lb)

- Green onions finely sliced (1 bunch)

- Jalapeno pepper diced (1)

- Tortilla chips (1 bag)

- Cheddar cheese grated (2 cups)

- Tomato sliced (1)

- Iceberg lettuce chopped (2 cups)

- Taco sauce or salsa for serving

Instructions

1. Cook ground beef in a cast-iron pan over moderate heat (using the grill, a bonfire or a gas stove) until it is no longer raw.

2. Make a hole in the middle of the beef and insert the jalapenos and the green onions. Cook, with a constant stirring for approximately five minutes.

3. Shift the mixture to the bowl and cover the bottom of the heated skillet with the chips.

4. Place the ground meat onion mixture uniformly over all the chips. Load with cheese, tomatoes, lettuce, and sauce. Dig in right away!

11 Foil pack french dip sandwiches

Ingredients

- Unsalted butter, melted to room temp. (1/2 cup)

- Au jus gravy mix, separated (1 pack)

- Worcestershire sauce (1 tsp.)

- Garlic dried and minced (3/4 tsp.)

- Onion powder (1/2 tsp.)

- Heavy-duty foil

- Baguettes (2 smaller)

- Deli roast beef (1 pound)

- Pre-sliced provolone cheese (12 slices)

Instructions

1. Preheat the barbecue grill to medium-high heat (400 degrees) or the oven to the 400 degrees F.

2. Start by preparing a mixture of butter. In a bowl, mix the softened unmelted butter, Worcestershire sauce, 1 tbsp of the au jus gravy mixture, the dried chopped garlic and the onion powder. Stir until the components are fully combined and set it aside.

3. Slice the baguette into equal sections of around 6 to 10 inches long.

4. First, prepare an ODD of small strips (roughly 1/2 inch big) in each strip of baguette, cutting just around 3/4 of the way through.

5. It is necessary to have an ODD number of slices so that each of the sandwiches has two slices of bread.

6. Divide the butter mixture produced in step two into two equal portions. Spread a small portion of the mixture within each slice of bread using a butter knife. Keep half of the mixture for the next time.

7. Slice each piece of the cheese in half and put one piece, along with one piece of roast meat, in-between each of the pieces of bread. (After all, these are actual pull-apart sandwiches, so you

don't want cheese and beef in-between every slice of bread).

8. Get the other half of a butter mixture and spread it over each sandwich's surface and sides with a pastry brush.

9. Cover every other baguette section in foil. Be sure that none of the slices is uncovered.

10. Put in the preheated oven for ten minutes or in the preheated grill for 6-10 min or until the bread is toasted and the cheese is melted.

11. If the baguette is thicker, it'll take more time.

12. Prepare the au jus as the sandwiches are grilling. Take the leftover mixture of au jus and put it in a medium saucepan over moderate flame.

13. Put two cups of ice water and stir. Bring to a simmer and lower the heat, enabling it to thicken gradually. (You can do it on the side stove of a skillet or also on the campfire, or you could just prepare at home

14. Lift the foil packs from the grill and open them cautiously to let the steam release. Pull the sandwiches apart and indulge in the au jus sauce

12 Greek lamb burgers with the dill potatoes

Ingredients

- ground lamb (1/2 lb)

- Ground coriander (1/4 tsp.)

- Ground beef (1/2 lb)

- ground cumin (1/4 tsp.)

- Ground nutmeg (1/4 tsp.)

- Garlic powder, divided (1/2 tsp.)

- Onion powder (1/4tsp.)

- kosher salt for taste

- Fresh oregano, diced (2 tsp.)

- cracked pepper for taste

- baby gold potatoes, diced (2 cups)

- Butter (3 tsp.)

- fresh dill, diced (1 tsp.)

- feta cheese (1 cup)

- tomatoes, diced (1 cup)

Instructions

1. Arrange a hot campfire and put a grill on top of it. Add a 9-12 inch cast iron pan over medium flame.

2. Pat the lamb and ground meat dry and add the cumin, cilantro, 1/4 teaspoon of garlic powder, onion powder, ground, nutmeg and fresh oregano to a pot.

3. Sprinkle with pepper and salt and blend well.

4. Shape four identical patties by your hand, and then press the dip into the middle of each one. Cover it and put back.

5. Apply the butter to the pan and let it melt. Saute in the sliced potatoes and simmer until they are crisp about ten minutes.

6. Season with salt, pepper and the leftover garlic powder.

7. Push the potatoes softly to the sides of the pan and nestle in the four meat burger patties.

8. Enable to cook on either side for five minutes or until cooked completely. Garnish potatoes with the fresh dill, and then finish with sliced tomatoes and the feta cheese.

13 Sausage and Egg Taquitos Breakfast

Ingredients

- Large eggs (5)

- Fresh black pepper and salt

- Fully cooked sausage (7-ounce box)

- Baby spinach leaves, chopped (1 cup)

- Shredded cheese (1 1/2 cups)

- White corn tortillas (10),

- Or use 6" flour tortillas.

Instructions

1. Oven preheated to 425° F.

2. Put the preserved sausage links over a moderate flame in a large frying pan. Cook, frequently turning, until fully warmed.

3. Place it on a plate and leave a little bit of the sausage fat in the pan.

4. Crack the eggs and add the splash of milk or water to the bowl. With a fork, whisk well and then transfer it to the pan.

5. Season with pepper and salt Cook, flipping and scrambling while they cook, for another few minutes. (if using spinach, put it in the pan around 2 minutes before the eggs are finished frying) Turn off the heat.

6. Heat the tortillas for a few seconds on a hot pan or griddle before they are pliable.

7. Spread the scrambled eggs on the tortillas and garnish with the melted cheese.

8. On top, position the sausage link. Roll-up and put on the baking sheet lined with parchment paper or foil, seam side down.

9. Use cooking spray to gently spray and bake for about 10-15 minutes on each side. For dipping, serve with the salsa.

14 Campfire Pizza

Ingredients

- Mozzarella cheese (2 cups)

- Pizza dough (frozen) or refrigerated pizza dough (1 tube)

- Pepperoni mushrooms of your choice,

- Vegetable toppings, whatever you want!
- Pizza sauce (1 jar)

Instructions

1. 1 Oil the cast-iron skillet (or pizza stone, baking tray, etc.)
2. Take the frozen dough and spread it in a pan.
3. Put on a grill or a barbecue. Grill until the bottom is golden brown.
4. Pull the crust from the fire and flip it in the frying pan.
5. Spread pizza sauce, put the toppings and top it with the cheese.
6. Return to flame and cook till the crust is done below and the toppings soft.
7. Serve and indulge it!

15 Campfire Cheese and Hot Ham Sandwiches

Ingredients

- Deli-sliced ham (1 lb)
- Swiss or Provolone cheese (12 slices)
- Hawaiian rolls (12)
- Melted butter (1/2 cup)
- Dried onion (1 tsp.)
- Dijon mustard (1 1/2 tsp.)
- Brown sugar (1 tsp.)

Instructions:

1. Start preparing Six heavy foil sheets.
2. Divide ham among twelve rolls. Place the cheese slice on top of the ham, then put a top roll on the top of the ham.
3. On every piece of foil put two sandwiches.

4. Mix the melted butter, onion, Dijon, and brown sugar. Gush it on the sandwiches uniformly over the top.

5. Fold up each packet's sides and shut them down. On heated campfire charcoals, put the packages.

6. Cook, occasionally turn till the cheese melts, and the rolls are gently toasted for 10-fifteen mins.

16 Cast iron frittata

Ingredients

- Milk (½ cup)

- Freshly ground pepper (¼ tsp.)

- thinly sliced shallot (1)

- Chopped basil (¼ cup)

- Large eggs (8)

- Sea salt (½ tsp.)

- Olive oil, in portions (2 tsp.)

- Cherry tomatoes (1 pint)

- Sliced Gruyere cheese (½ cup)

Instructions

1. Get a campfire or the coal prepared for cooking.

2. Beat the eggs, milk, salt and black pepper together in a mixing bowl until fully combined. Just set aside.

3. Heat 1 tbsp of oil over the moderate flame in a 10" pan. Include the shallot and start sautéing for 7-ten minutes before soft and browning occurs.

4. By lifting the campfire grater or shifting the skillet to the barbecue's cold side, minimize the heat to the medium-low.

5. To the skillet, add the onions, accompanied by the basil, egg mixture and cheese. Cap with a lid. Scatter around the lid some embers.

6. Cook for about fifteen minutes until the frittata has become puffy, and the eggs are almost set (check every ten minutes to check progress, use a heatproof glove or even a lid lifter to raise the lid).

7. Serve and eat it with extra cheese and basil if wanted!

17 Dutch oven Cornbread and Chili

Ingredients

For the Chili

- Oil (1 tablespoon)

- Salt (2 teaspoons)

- Ground cumin (1 teaspoon)

- Can kidney beans, drained (14.5 oz)

- Can diced green chilies (4 oz)

- Medium onion, diced (1)

- Garlic cloves, minced (4)

- Chili powder (1-2 teaspoons)

- Can black beans, drained (14.5 oz)

- Can diced tomatoes (14.5 oz)

- Tomato paste (2 tablespoons)

For the Topping of Cornbread

- Flour (½ cup)

- Salt (1 ½ tsp.)

- Lightly beaten egg (1)

- Cornmeal (1 cup)

- Honey (2 tsp.)

- Milk (1 cup)

- Baking powder (1 tsp.)

Instructions

1. Stir fry the onion in oil for around 5 minutes in a 10' / 4 qt Dutch oven over a moderate flame until soft and only starting to turn golden.

2. Include the spices and garlic and simmer for 1 minute. Mix the chilies, beans, and tomato puree and stir. Simmer till it thickens, for ten minutes.

3. Meanwhile, make the batter for the cornbread. In a wide bowl, mix all of the dried ingredients and stir to blend.

4. Include the egg, milk, and honey and whisk until it forms the batter.

5. Shift the Dutch oven on indirect fire to minimize bubbling.

6. Pour the batter as uniformly as possible on the chili, close the Dutch oven with the lid and place coals and embers on top of the lid.

7. Go for an approximate temperature between 400-425F.

8. Bake for around 20 minutes till the cornbread has cooked completely and is no further moist in the middle. Serve & enjoy with your choice of chili toppings!

18 Baked Wrapped Sweet Potatoes and Chili

Ingredients

- Sliced onion (1)

- Can tomato paste (6 oz)

- Can kidney beans, washed (15 oz)

- Beer can (½)

- Chili powder (1 tsp.)

- Salt (½ tsp.)

- **Cumin** (½ tbsp.)

- Large sweet potatoes (4)

- Olive oil (1 tbsp.)

- Green onions, avocado or cheese for garnish

Instructions

1. Cover each one of the sweet potatoes in heavy foil and nestle them in the flames of the campfire.

2. To make sure they cook uniformly, flip them every so often.

3. Prepare the chili when the potatoes are being cooked.

4. Preheat in the pan over a low flame. When heated, add ¾ of the sliced onions (keep half for garnish) and fry for a few minutes before they begin to soften.

5. Corn, tomato paste, beer (or other fluid, such as broth), and spices are added. Mix well to combine for 15-20 minutes

6. Remove from the fire when the potatoes are tender and cooked properly (approximately 30 minutes max, give or take a little bit based on their size). Carefully remove the foil.

7. To make a slit into the potato, make use of a knife and garnish it with the onions, chilies and whatever else may have on the side. Savor!

19 Grilled Mexican street corn

Ingredients

- Ears corn (4)

- Juice of a lime (1/2)

- Mayo (1/2 cup)

- Salt (1/2 tsp.)

- A handful of chopped cilantro

- Chili powder (1 tsp.)

- crumbled cojita, (1/2 cup)

Instructions

1. Prepare the corn by removing the husks' peel (without cutting them from the bottom) and extracting all the silk. Remove the husks.

2. Place your corn on the grate of the campfire.

3. Grill, stirring regularly, till the corn has been charred and cooked evenly for 10-15 minutes.

4. Lift it from the grill and let it cool down a bit so that it's easy to treat. Please take off the husks and dispose of them.

5. In a clean bowl, add the mayonnaise, lime juice, salt and chili powder.

6. Pour evenly all over the corn. Sprinkle on the top with the cojita and cilantro.

7. Serve and indulge!

Chapter 5: Dinner recipes

1. Red Wine Poached Short Ribs with Parsnip Celery Root Sauce

Ingredients

For prep of the short ribs

- Meaty short ribs, four big pieces, extra fat trimmed, (3 lbs)

- Olive oil (1 tablespoon)

- Pepper and kosher salt

- Stalk celery, chopped (1)

- Large fresh thyme (1)

- Medium carrot scrubbed not peeled, chopped (1)

- Cloves of garlic, finely chopped (6)

- Large onion, chopped (1)

- Flour (use gluten-free flour) (2 tbsp.)

- Tomato paste (1 tbsp.)

- Water (2 cups)

- Dry red wine (1 1/2 cups)

- Bay leaves (2)

For making the celery root + parsnip sauce:

- Parsnips (3 medium), peeled and cubed (1 1/4 – 1 1/2 lbs)

- Butter (4 tbsp.)

- Celery root, peeled and cubed (1 1/4 – 1 1/2 lb)

- Whole milk (substitute non-dairy milk for paleo) (1/2 – 1 cup)

- To taste used white pepper

- To taste, use kosher salt

Instructions

1. Take the short ribs out from the fridge, season them well with salt and pepper on both sides, then let them rest for at least thirty minutes at room temperature before actually cooking

2. Heat the oven to 325 degrees. * Adding olive oil over high temperature to a wide Dutch oven, then place the short ribs slowly in the hot oil.

3. Let simmer until fully browned (about 5 minutes), then flip and cook the remaining sides. Don't owe this move hurry.

4. To attain the best taste, ensure the ribs are caramelized on all ends. Remove and let it sit on a dish to absorb all the liquids.

5. Drain and add one tsp of oil and include the celery, carrots and onion.

6. Reduce the heat and simmer for around 8 minutes, frequently stirring, until tender.

7. Add the cloves of garlic and keep on cooking for another 8 minutes before the vegetables appear slightly brown.

8. Put the tomato puree and mix for around 3-4 minutes before it is caramelized. Add flour and cook until entirely absorbed, for 1-two minutes.

9. To scrape off all the bits sticking to the plate's bottom, add the red wine and use a wooden spoon.

10. Add the bay leaves, the water, the thyme, and let it boil.

11. Put the short ribs along with their juices back in the tub, and then spoon some of the liquid and vegetables over the end. For 1 1/2 hours, cover and put in the oven.

12. Remove any fat that's going to collect on the surface.

13. If it gets dry, turn the short ribs to the other side and transfer a little more water to the pan.

    Cook for 1 1/2 to 2 hours or when the meat falls off the bone. Skim off all the excess fat from the oven, then let it stay in the pot while preparing the parsnip puree and celery root

14. Add the celery root and the parsnips to a medium saucepan and cover with cool water.

15. Boil, then start reducing to the simmer and cook for around 15-20 minutes until tender.

16. Drain and allow stay for a few moments to dry in the saucepan (too much moisture will dilute the puree).

17. Along with all the butter and 1/2 cup of milk, transfer the veggies back to the pot. To make puree creamy, use an electric mixer.

18. Similarly, you may achieve this in a food processor or mixer, but the electric mixer makes it that much simpler. I don't suggest hand grinding because you're not going to get a texture that good.

19. Add a little extra milk at a time until it reaches the required consistency.

20. To taste, season with black pepper and salt.

21. To taste seasoned, it took up an entire tbsp of salt for me, but don't be shy (the exact quantity would rely on whether you chose salted butter or not and if so, which brand).

22. To eat, put a huge amount of celery root and parsnip purée on a serving plate or bowl, top with the short rib and a spoonful of sauce on top.

2 Slow-cooked orange bbq ribs and bourbon

Ingredients

- Pork ribs cleaved into pieces (3 lb)

- Shots bourbon (4)

- Barbecue sauce of your choice (2 cups)

- The juice of large navel oranges (2)

- Fresh thyme (2 tsp)

- Orange slices (4-5)

- Garlic powder (1 tbsp)

- Salt and pepper to taste

- Seasoning salt (2 tsp)

Instructions

1. Combine barbecue sauce, orange juice, bourbon, orange slices and thyme in a medium dish. Put it aside.

2. Season the ribs with seasoning salt, garlic powder and black pepper.

3. Put the ribs in the Crock-Pot Express Crock and cover with the sauce.

4. Click SLOW COOK, set the temperature to Maximum, and set the time to 4 hours. Please ensure the Steam Escape Valve is in the "Release" button. Push START/STOP.

5. After cooking is over, move to the serving plate and serve warm.

6. Cherish it!

3 Slow cooked chicken breast with hot gravy

Ingredients

- Olive oil, divided into portions (2 tbsp.)

- Salt and black pepper to taste

- Skinless, boneless chicken breasts (6)

- Chicken broth (1 cup)

- Chopped parsley (2 tbsp.)

- Italian seasoning (2 tsp.)

- Balsamic vinegar (2 tbsp.)

- Soy sauce (1/4 cup)

- Brown sugar (2 tbsp.)

- Cornstarch (2 tbsp.)

- Minced garlic (2 tsp.)

- Butter (1 tbsp.)

Instructions

1. Heat 1 tsp of olive oil in a frying pan over moderate flame.

2. Season chicken breasts with black pepper, salt and Italian seasoning on all sides.

3. Simmer chicken 4-5 minutes per side or until lightly browned.

4. Put the chicken in a slow cooker.

5. In a medium bowl, combine the remaining tsp of olive oil, soy sauce, chicken broth, balsamic vinegar, brown sugar and garlic.

6. Add the sauce to the chicken.

7. Cover the slow cooker and cook LOW for 4-5 hours or HIGH for 2-three hours.

8. Take the chicken from the slow cooker, put it on a plate, cover it with foil to stay warm.

9. In a pot, drain the liquid out of the slow cooker. Heat the pot on moderate flame and bring the liquid to a boil.

10. Blend the cornstarch with 1/4 of a cup of cool water. Add cornstarch to the pot and then get to a boil.

11. Cook for two minutes or until the sauce has slightly thickened.

12. Put the butter in the pot and whisk until it is melted. Take the pot out from the heat.

13. Cut or chop the chicken and pour that sauce over that chicken. Garnish with the parsley, serve.

4 Slow Cooker Black-Eyed Peas

Ingredients

- Three cans of un-drained black-eyed-peas (15 ounces)

- large onion, diced (1)

- Garlic powder for seasoning

- Boneless pork chops (1.5 pounds)

- Salt and black pepper to taste

Instructions

1. Open and dump the three cans of black-eyed peas into a slow cooker and season to taste with pepper and salt.

2. Sprinkle the pork chops on both corners with garlic powder, salt and pepper. Put in a uniform layer placed above the black-eyed peas in a slow cooker.

3. Cover the prepared pork chops with the sliced onion in a uniform layer. Season to taste with some more pepper and salt if you want to

4. Put the cover on a slow cooker and cook at a lower flame for six to eight hours or at a higher flame for two to four hours based on the slow cooker you are using. Occasionally lift the lid to stir.

5. Test the pork chops for the perfect flavor and texture until the time is almost over. End up serving over the rice with the south cornbread as aside.

5 Thai spicy Chicken Curry {Instant Pot /Slow Cooker}
Ingredients

- 14 oz can of coconut milk (1)

- Red curry paste, such as thai chicken or mae ploy (3 tbsp)

- Chicken broth low-sodium (1/2 cup)

- Brown sugar (1 tsp)

- Ground cumin (1/2 tsp)

- Ground coriander (1/2 tsp.)

- Peeled and chopped ginger (1 tbsp.)

- Salt to taste

- Peeled and chopped garlic (2 tsp.)

- Skinless, boneless chicken breasts (1 1/2 lbs)

- Medium yellow onion, thinly diced (1/2)

- Three medium diced carrots (1 1/2 cups)

- Stalk lemongrass, cut into four pieces and outer layer removed (1)

- Creamy peanut butter (2 tbsp.)

- Large red bell pepper, sliced (1)

- Fresh lime juice (1 tbsp.)

- Chopped cilantro, divide into portions (1/4 cup)

- Unsalted peanuts, chopped for serving (1/3 cup)

- Fish sauce (1 tbsp.)

- Cooked brown rice or jasmine rice, for serving

Instructions

1. Stir together the coconut milk, red curry paste, chicken broth, brown sugar, cumin, cilantro, ginger and garlic in the 5 - 7-quart slow cooker. Season gently, with the salt (about 1/4 tsp).

2. To cook slowly in the slow cooker, incorporate carrots, chicken, onions and immerse lemongrass in the broth.

3. Place the lid and cook on low flame for around five hours unless the chicken is cooked evenly and soft, including bell pepper in the cooker's last 45 minutes.

4. Take the chicken from the slow cooker and allow it to sit for a few minutes before shredding. Remove the lemongrass, as is required.

5. In the slow cooker, blend the peanut butter, the lime juice and the fish sauce, and then add the chicken and half of the cilantro.

6. Season to taste with a bit more salt (I needed a further 1/4 teaspoon of salt). Serve hot with rice and garnish with cilantro and peanuts.

6 Crockpot baked potatoes

Ingredients

- Russet potatoes (4-6)

- Olive oil (2-3 tsp), per potato (1/2 tsp.)

- Kosher salt (1-1.5 tsp.), per potato (1/4 tsp.)

- Aluminum foil

- Butter, chives, cheese, bacon, salt, sour cream and pepper

Instructions

1. Rinse and dry potatoes, and use a fork to prick the potatoes.

2. Put each potato in the middle of a piece of aluminum foil that is wide enough to cover the potato completely.

3. Rub both sides of each potato with 1/2 teaspoon of olive oil and 1/4 teaspoon of kosher salt.

4. Cover the foil firmly all around the potatoes and put them in the Crockpot.

5. Cook on Higher flame for 4-5 hours or on a Lower flame for 8-10 hours till soft. Make sure you're not overcooking them.

6. When finished, withdraw it from the Crockpot and gently remove the foil.

7. Slice each of the potatoes in half lengthwise and cover with your preferred butter, chips, cheese, sour cream, bacon, salt and pepper or your other ideal topping. Enjoy it!

7 Sweet n Sour Chicken

Ingredients

- Large orange (1)

- Red wine vinegar (1/4 cup)

- Dark brown sugar can pack (1)

- Kosher salt to taste

- Chicken legs (4)

- Pepper to taste

- All-purpose flour (2 tbsp.)

- Large red onion (1)

- Fresh flat-leaf parsley (1/2 cup)

- White rice, Long-grained (1 cup)

- Cloves of garlic (6)

- Can of peach halves (1 cup)

Instructions

1. Remove two strips of zest from the orange with a vegetable peeler.

2. Cut the zest thinly. Juice the orange into the 5-to 6-qt slow cooker (you can get around 1/2 cups). Stir in sugar, vinegar, 3/4 tsp of salt and 1/4 tsp of pepper.

3. Mix the chicken with flour, and then add the garlic and orange zest to the slow cooker. Spread the onion on the top.

4. Cook, sealed, unless the chicken is cooked evenly and the sauce is lightly thickened, seven to eight hours on low flame or 5 to 6 hours on the elevated flame.

5. Thirty minutes before you serve, prepare the rice in the box instructions.

6. When the rice is almost done preparing, move the chicken to either a plate or tray.

7. Transfer the peaches to the slow cooker and simmer for about 3 minutes, sealed, until cooked through; fold in the parsley.

8. Spoon the blend of peach and onion on the chicken and eat with the rice.

8 Slow cooker smoky beef tacos

Ingredients

- Can of tomato sauce (8-ounce)

- Flank steak, cut crosswise into two 1/2-inch-wide pieces (1 3/4 lb.)

- Chipotle in adobo, chopped (1 tbsp.)

- Ground cumin (2 tsp.)

- Adodo sauce (1 tbsp.)

- Kosher salt to taste

- Red onion, thinly diced (1)

- Cloves of garlic, minced (4)

- Corn tortillas, pico de gallo and sour cream, for serving

Instructions

1. In the 5-to-6-quarter slow cooker, mix tomato sauce, adobo sauce, chipotle, cumin and 1/2 tsp salt. Mix in the garlic, the onion, and the steak.

2. Cover the cooker and cook until beef is juicy, 4 to 5 hours high or 7 to 8 hours on low flame. Shred meat with two forks.

3. Serve with sour cream, tortillas, and pico de gallo on the side.

9 Crockpot ribs

Ingredients

- Large onion (1)

- Water (½ cup)

- Baby back ribs, two pieces (3-4 lbs)

- Cloves of garlic (4)

- Ketchup (¼ cup)

- Favorite bbq sauce (½ cup)

- Bbq rib sauce

- **Chili sauce** (½ cup)

Instructions

1. Combine all the ingredients (below).

2. Pull the silver membrane from the back of the ribs. Rub the front and back of the ribs with a blend of spices.

3. Put the onion, chopped garlic, the water and the ribs in a slow cooker.

4. Cook the ribs for 4 hours on high heat or 8 hours on low heat or until the rib is soft.

5. Preheat the broiler.

6. Combine ketchup with chili sauce and the barbecue sauce.

7. Brush the ribs with the mix of sauce and sauté (or grill) for 3-5 minutes or till scorched.

10 Slow cooker melt in mouth bbq chicken

Ingredients

- Skinless, boneless chicken breasts (3 pounds)

- Molasses (1/3 cup)

- Ketchup (1 cup)

- Brown sugar (1/3 cup)

- Worcestershire sauce (1 tbsp.)

- Cider vinegar (3 tbsp.)

- Smoked paprika (1 tsp.)

- Chili powder (1 tsp.)

- Salt (1/2 tsp.)

- Onion powder (1 tsp.)

- Water (2 tbsp.)

- Liquid smoke (2 tsp.)

- Cornstarch (1 tbsp.)

Instructions

1. Place the chicken at the bottom of the slow cooker. In a large bowl, stir together ketchup, molasses, white vinegar, brown sugar Worcestershire sauce, chili powder, paprika, onion powder, liquid smoke and salt.

2. Drizzle the sauce over the chicken and simmer on low heat for 4-6 hours or on high heat for 3-4 until it is soft enough to shred.

3. Shred chicken and combine cornstarch with water.

4. Add it to the bbq sauce and then let the sauce thicken for another 30 minutes.

11 Slow cooker pork chops

Ingredients

- An envelope of ranch dressing mix (1)

- Pork chops, bone out (1 pound)

- Pepper (1/2 teaspoon)

- Garlic powder (1/2 teaspoon)

- An envelope of brown gravy mix (1)

- Beef broth (1 1/2 cups)

- Water (2 tablespoons)

- Can of cream of chicken soup (10.5 ounces)

- Cornstarch (2 tablespoons)

Instructions

1. Season the pork chops with a ranch dressing blend, garlic powder and pepper on both sides.

2. In the big, slow cooker, stir the brown gravy mixture, beef broth and cream of chicken soup.

3. Add to the slow cooker the seasoned pork chops.

4. Cover and simmer for 6-7 hours at low heat or 3-four hours at high heat.

5. Carefully extract the pork chops from the slow cooker on a plate.

6. In a shallow bowl, combine cornstarch and water. add the corn starch mixture to the Crockpot to make the gravy thick

7. End up serving over the rice or mashed potatoes and, if desired, garnish with parsley.

12 One-Pot Pasta

Ingredients

For the kale

- Head kale, diced and de-stemmed (1)

- Salt (½ teaspoon)

- Olive oil (1 tablespoon)

- Cloves of garlic, minced (2)

- Red pepper flakes (1 pinch)

For the pasta

- Lentil pasta (10 oz)

- One jar of tomato sauce (23 oz)

- Water (2 cups)

- Cheese, remove if making the vegan recipe (1/4 cup)

Instructions

Cook the kale

1. Heat 1 tbsp of olive oil and red pepper flakes over a moderate flame in a high-sided skillet.

2. Once the oil is warmed, add the garlic, kale, salt, and toss until the kale is soft.

3. Take the kale from the pan and put it aside.

4. Prepare the pasta:

5. In a pan, add tomato sauce and water and rise to a simmer.

6. Add the pasta to the pan and cook for the specified time on the box or until pasta is done, stirring regularly to ensure that the pasta is cooked accurately.

7. Whisk the cooked kale in the sauce to warm and take the pan off the flame.

8. Assemble and eat: Spread cheese on the top and serve.

13 Cheesy Asparagus One Pot Orzo

Ingredients

- Asparagus (1/2 lb)

- Orzo (1 cup)

- Water (2 cups)

- Olive oil (1/2 tablespoon)

- Dried basil (1/2 teaspoon)

- Dried thyme (1/2 teaspoon)

- Garlic powder (1/2 teaspoon)

- Red pepper flakes (1/4 teaspoon)

- Salt (1/2 teaspoon)

- Sun-dried tomatoes, chopped (1/4 cup)

- Pine nuts (2 tablespoons)

- Shredded cheese, you could use parmesan, or any blend (1/2 cup)

Instructions

1. Cut off and waste the asparagus' rough ends, then chop the asparagus into 1" small pieces.

2. Add the asparagus, the water, the orzo, the oil and all the spices to the bath. Bring to a low boil (it took us 4 1/2 mins) and simmer for another 5 minutes till the orzo is soft.

3. Reduce flame and include cheese, pine nuts and sun-dried tomatoes. Stir till the cheese is melted.

4. Remove from flame, season with salt and pepper to taste, and enjoy!

14 Campfire grill Cornbread

Ingredients

- Cornmeal, ground (1 cup)

- Baking powder (1 tablespoon)

- Flour (1/2 cup)

- Salt (1/2 teaspoon)

- Large egg (1)

- Milk (1 cup)

- Dry milk powder (3 tbsp.)

- Honey (2 tablespoons)

- Oil (1/2 tablespoon)

Instructions

1. In a big bowl, add the cornmeal, baking powder, flour and salt and mix.

2. Add the egg, milk, and honey to dry ingredients. Blend with a fork until fully combined.

3. Heat the oil in your cast iron skillet over your campfire. Swirl to cover the bottom (make sure to use anything to shield you from heat.

4. The skillet will get hot!). Pour the mixture into the skillet, ensuring that it is properly layered. Wrap the skillet with foil, sealing the foil around the rim, or cover with the lid.

5. Cook over medium heat for fifteen minutes, remove the heat and allow the bread to rest (still covered) for another five minutes.

6. Cut bread into slices and eat with a huge bowl of chili!

15 Slow Cooker Chicken with Mango Salsa {with Coconut Rice}

Ingredients

- Mango salsa chicken

- Skinless, boneless chicken breasts (1 1/2 lbs)

- Chili powder (1/2 tsp.)

- Ground cumin (1 tsp.)

- Ground coriander (1/2 tsp.)

- Two minced cloves of garlic (2 tsp.)

- Paprika (1/2 tsp.)

- Freshly grounded pepper and salt

- A can of black beans washed and drained (15 oz)

- A jar of mango peach salsa (16 oz)

- Fresh lime juice (1 tbsp.)

- One slice of mango (optional)

- Frozen corn (1 1/4 cups)

- Chopped cilantro (1/4 cup)

- large avocado, diced (1)

- Coconut rice

- Jasmine rice, properly washed and drained (1 1/2 cups)

- Canned coconut milk with full fat, shaken well (1 1/4 cups)

- Coconut water or plain water (1 1/2 cups)

Instructions

1. For the chicken mango salsa

2. Place the chicken breasts in a 5-6 quarter slow cooker uniformly.

3. Sprinkle with the cumin, paprika, chili powder, coriander and garlic. Season with pepper and

salt.

4. Pour salsa uniformly over the chicken. Cover the slow cooker and cook for five hours at low heat or till chicken is readily cooked and shredded.

5. Take out the chicken from the slow cooker and pass it to the cutting board. Leave the mixture of salsa in the cooker.

6. Add the black beans and the corn to the salsa, cover and simmer over high heat for around five minutes.

7. Shred the chicken and return to a slow cooker with lime juice and cilantro; toss the mixture gently.

8. Serve warm with avocados and mangos over coconut rice.

9. Rinse under warm water in a metal mesh sieve and drain to defrost corn easily.

10. For coconut rice

11. Bring coconut water, rice, coconut milk, and 1/2 teaspoon salt to a boil in a wide skillet over medium heat.

12. Cover and minimize to low heat. Simmer approximately 20 minutes until liquid is absorbed. Just let it rest for ten minutes.

16 Parmesan Herb Baked Salmon Fillet

Ingredients:

- Melted butter (2 tbsp.)

- Salmon fillet (1 1b.)

- Lemon juice (2 tsp.)

- Grated Parmesan cheese (1/4 cup)

- Italian seasoned breadcrumbs (1/4 cup)

- Minced fresh basil (2 tsp.) / Dried basil (3/4 tsp.)

Instructions:

1. Preheat the oven to 375 ° F.

2. Spray a baking sheet with cooking spray (for easy cleaning, if needed, line with foil).

3. Place the salmon on the prepared baking sheet (skin side down).

4. Stir the melted butter and lemon juice together in a small bowl. Brush the salmon with half of the butter mixture.

5. To the remaining melted butter mixture, add breadcrumbs, Parmesan cheese, and basil. Stir to blend together.

6. Press the buttered breadcrumbs gently onto the fish with your fingers.

7. Bake for 12-18 minutes or golden brown before the salmon flakes easily with a fork and topping (total cooking time can differ based on the fish's thickness).

17 Poached Salmon

Ingredients:

- Dry white wine (1 ½ cups)

- Water (1 cup)

- 3 lemon slices

- Onion, peeled & cut in half (1)

- Sprigs dill (5)/ dried dill (2 tsp.)

- Sprigs parsley (5)/ dried parsley (2 tsp.)

- Sprigs thyme (5)/dried thyme (2 tsp.)

- Peeled Whole garlic cloves (3)

- Salt (1 tsp.)

- Fresh boneless skinless salmon fillet (1 1b.)

- Garnish: sliced lemon, lemon zest, or fresh herbs chopped

Instructions:

1. Combine the wine, sugar, lemon slices, dill, parsley, onion, garlic, thyme, and salt in a medium

skillet or saucepan. Just bring it to a boil.

2. Reduce the liquid over low heat to a boil. The salmon is added then cover.

3. Cook for five to eight minutes before the salmon is cooked.

4. For serving dishes, remove the salmon.

5. Garnish, if necessary, with chopped herbs and fresh lemon zest.

18 Baja Style Fish Tacos

Ingredients:

- Eggs (2)

- Flour (1/2 cup)

- Panko bread crumbs (1 cup)

- Snapper fillets / other mild, white fish (1/2 pound)

- Salt (1 tsp.)

- Grapeseed /other neutral-flavored) oil (1/2 cup)

- Tortillas (6-8 corn)

- Earthbound Farm Organic Southwest Chopped Salad Kit (1 package)

- Lime, quartered (1)

- Red onion and additional cilantro, finely chopped optional

Instructions:

1. Prep the breading station: In a small bowl, crack the eggs and beat them together. On two plates (or two sides of one large plate), spread the flour and the panko.

2. Bread the fish: Cut the fish fillets into slices measuring 1⁄2-3⁄4 inches. Sprinkle the tops with salt. Dredge each piece in flour, dip to coat in the egg, leave to drip off the excess, and then coat in panko. Place aside

3. Fry the fish: Line a paper towel with a plate. In a high-sided pan, heat around 1⁄2 cup of neutral-flavored oil. Until the oil is heated, one piece at a time, add the fish. Fry until the bread is golden

and the fish is cooked on either side for 30-60 seconds. When they finish cooking, take the fish and place them on the lined plate.

4. Assemble the tacos: On your stove or over a campfire, warm the tortillas. Lay down a bed of greens from the salad kit to build the tacos, add a piece or two fried fish, and top with some of the tomatillo dressing, squeeze of lime, onions and additional cilantro added.

5. Serve & enjoy!

19 Tin Foil Seafood Boil

Ingredients:

- 1 lemon (sliced in eight rounds)

- Olive oil

- 16 shrimp, deveined and peeled (3/4 lb)

- 8 sea scallops (1/2 lb)

- 2 ears corn

- 8 (new/fingerling) potatoes, halved or quartered (3/4 lb)

- Andouille sausage 3 (cut in ¼" slices)

- Dry white wine, beer 1 cup/chicken broth

- Butter (1/4 cup)

Instructions:

1. On high heat, prepare a grill.

2. Spray lightly with oil on aluminum foil four sheets. Divide the shrimp, lemon, scallops, beans, potatoes, and bacon, stacking the products in the middle. To form a bowl, bring up all four sides of the foil.

3. Onto each box, pour an equivalent quantity of beer (wine/broth), followed by some butter pats and Old Bay seasoning sprinkle. Fold the foil on top tightly, allowing room for steam & heat to circulate within the package.

4. For around 15 mins, grill the packets till the seafood is cooked and the veggies are tender.

20   Artichoke and Poblano Campfire Paella

Ingredients:

- Olive or vegetable oil (2 tbsp.)

- 2-4 sausages (Tofurky Italian style)

- Poblano peppers (2)

- Green onions (3)

- Large shallot, diced (1)

- Cloves garlic, roughly chopped (3)

- Rice (1/2 cup)

- Tempranillo 1/4 cup (other medium-bodied red wine)

- Broth (14 oz) cup

- Salt (1/2 tsp.)

- Pinch of saffron

- Artichoke hearts, drained and halved (14 oz) cup

Instructions:

1. Place the poblanos, green onions, and sausage over the fire directly on the pan, occasionally turning until the peppers and onions are soft and crispy, and much of the sausage is cooked through. Remove it from your grill. Slice the sausage into pieces of around 1/4 inch. Allow the peppers to cool, extract the seeds, peel off the skin, and chop. Chop the green onions into bite-sized bits. Only set aside.

2. Place the cast iron skillet directly over the fire on the grill. To cover the bottom of the skillet, pour enough oil and then add the shallots. Saute for 3-5 minutes until it is soft. Add the sliced sausage and garlic and saute for around 30 seconds until the garlic is fragrant. Add the rice and cook for 2-3 minutes, occasionally stirring, until the ends are just translucent. In the pan, pour 1/4 cup red wine, allow to evaporate, then add the broth. Add salt and a pinch of saffron to season. Stir well to distribute all the ingredients evenly, and then leave 20-30 minutes to simmer, undisturbed, until all the liquid is absorbed.

3. To reheat, add to the pan the chopped poblanos, green onions, and artichoke hearts. At this

point, the paella on the bottom will start developing the Socarrat. You can begin to hear the rice beginning to crackle after a few minutes. This is your indicator that the dish is almost done. To ensure that the Socarrat has developed, cook for a few more minutes (you can use a spoon to check a small portion of the pan).

4. Serve immediately, along with a glass of the remaining red wine, shared out of the skillet or served on individual plates.

21 Sweet & Savory Grilled Tempeh

Ingredients:

- Maple syrup (1/4 cup)

- Soy sauce (2 tbsp.)

- Apple cider vinegar (1 tbsp.)

- Tempeh (8 oz)

Instructions:

1. In a ziplock bag large enough to hold tempeh, mix the maple syrup, soy sauce, and apple cider vinegar.

2. Cut the tempeh into 4 pieces. With the marinade, place them in the ziplock. Ensure that the slices of tempeh are uniformly coated and allow for at least 30 minutes to marinate.

3. Grill the tempeh over your campfire or cook it with a touch of oil in a cast-iron skillet. Cook on both sides for 2-3 minutes.

22 Campfire Tacos with Sweet Potato, Poblano Peppers & Black Beans

Ingredients:

Sweet potatoes

- Oil (1 tbsp.)

- Sweet potato (1) med, peeled cut in ½" cubes

- 1 poblano pepper (seeded & chopped in ½" pieces)

- Cumin (1 tbsp.)

- Salt

- Black beans

- Oil (1 tbsp.)

- Small diced red onion (1/2)

- Minced Cloves garlic (2)

- 15 oz cup black beans (1)

- Juiced (2 limes)

- Chili powder New Mexican (1 tsp.)

- Salt

Assembly

- Corn tortillas (6)

- Red onion, cilantro, hot sauce, avocado, etc. (1/2)

Instructions:

1. Heat one tbsp of oil over med-high heat in a skillet. Add the potatoes, then cook, stirring regularly, for 10 mins. Add the cumin, peppers, and salt and cook for another 10 mins or till the peppers and potatoes are fully cooked and soft.

2. Start preparing the black beans in the meantime. In a tiny pot, heat one tbsp of oil. Add the onion, then saute for 3-4 mins till it becomes translucent. Now add the garlic, then saute for around 1 min until it is fragrant. Now add the lime juice, beans, chili powder New Mexico and salt. Reduce the heat and simmer till the beans are cooked, and the peppers & potatoes are done for about 15 mins.

3. For assembly, cook the tortillas over the campfire either on the stove burner. Spoon into the tortilla a scoop of beans, add a scoop of peppers and potatoes, and cover with whatever extra fixings you'd want

23 Udon Noodle Salad with Tofu, Vegetables & Sesame Marinade

Ingredients:

Marinated Tofu

- 15 oz package of tofu (1)

- 2 Tamari (2 tbsp.)

- Garlic cloves pressed (2)

- Sesame oil/ extra virgin olive oil (1 tbsp.)

Udon Noodle Salad

- Package of whole wheat udon noodles (8 oz)

- Thinly sliced Red bell pepper, seeded (1 medium)

- Thinly sliced orange bell pepper, seeded (1 medium)

- 15 oz cup corn (1)

- Thinly sliced Small jicama (1)

- Thinly sliced Scallions, thinly sliced (2)

- 35 oz bag of roasted seaweed snacks (1)

- Sesame oil/extra virgin olive oil (2 tbsp.)

- Sea salt (1/2 tsp.)

- Dried red chili flakes (1 tsp.)

Sesame Dressing

- Cloves garlic pressed (2)

- Tamari (2 tbsp.)

- Brown rice vinegar (1/4 cup)

- Sesame seeds (2 tbsp.)

- Toasted sesame oil (1/4 cup plus 1 tbsp.)

- Chopped cilantro (1 cup)

Instructions:

Home

1. To remove excess liquid, rinse and drain the tofu by setting it in a strainer. Slice into small rectangles and lay in a shallow bowl.

2. Add the tamari and rub the pressed garlic with the tofu. Evenly coat the two sides.

3. For up to three days, tofu may remain covered in a fridge or cooler.

Camp

1. Boil the water in a large pot and add the udon noodles. Cook according to the package's directions or until tender. Drain and set aside the noodles. Rinse the noodles to stop them from sticking together once you have access to cool water. Otherwise, add to the pot a little sesame or extra virgin olive oil and mix it with the noodles.

2. Cut into thin slices of all the vegetables (bell pepper, jicama, scallion).

3. Over medium heat, warm oil in a cast iron or skillet. Add the peppers and scallions and saute for 8-10 minutes.

4. Stir in the salt and cook for another 5 minutes before adding the corn and jicama to the mixture. For another 5 minutes, cook all the ingredients together until the peppers are cooked through and begin to brown.

5. Sprinkle with sesame seeds, red chili flakes, and roasted seaweed and add the grilled vegetables to the bowl of noodles.

6. Reduce the heat to low on the cast iron and cook the marinated tofu for 5 minutes or until it is golden or brown. Flip the tofu and cook until golden, for an extra 4-5 minutes.

7. Add tofu to the salad and mix the sesame dressing with all the ingredients. Oh, Devour!

24 Five Ingredient Vegan Tacos

Ingredients:

- Water (3/4 cup)

- Dried minced onions (1/2 tbsp.)/Onion powder (1 tsp.)

- Taco seasoning (1 tbsp.)

- Textured vegetable protein (TVP) (1 cup)

- 15oz cup drained black beans (1)

- Salt

- Corn tortillas (6)

- Avocado, salsa, limes, cilantro, red onion (toppings) optional

Instructions:

1. Bring to a boil the water, onion, and taco seasoning. Add the TVP now and then reduce the heat to a low stage. Allow the liquid to be absorbed by the TVP, and now add the black drained beans.

2. Cover & cook on less heat till the tortillas are cooked, stirring regularly-be careful not to allow the filling to scorch on the pot bottom. Seasoning-if necessary, add salt (all taco seasonings have diff. salt content, so use the judgment of yours about Adding it how much).

3. In a pan with some oil, on a grill, or over the stove boiler, heat the tortillas.

4. From the heat, remove the filling and use your preferred toppings to make up your tacos.

25 Grilled Ratatouille Kebabs

Ingredients:

- Olive oil, divided (2 tbsp.)

- Small yellow onion, diced (1)

- Cloves garlic, minced (2-3)

- Tomatoes, finely chopped (1 pound)

- Chopped fresh oregano (1 tsp.)

- Chopped fresh basil (1 tsp.)

- Salt (1 tsp.)

- medium zucchini (about 1.5 lbs)

- medium yellow summer squash (about 1.5 lbs)

- 2 large Chinese eggplants (about 1 lb)

Instructions:

1. **Make the sauce:** Heat 1 tablespoon of olive oil over medium heat in a skillet until it shimmers. Attach the onion and cook until translucent and golden color is only beginning to take on. Add the garlic and sauté for around 30 seconds before it is fragrant. Mix well and add the chopped tomatoes, basil, oregano, and salt. Simmer over medium heat for around 20 minutes, stirring regularly, until the kebabs are cooked.

2. **Make the kebabs:** Meanwhile, slice the zucchini, squash, and eggplant into 1/2-inch-thick slices. Alternating each vegetable, assemble the kebabs on skewers. Drizzle with 1 tablespoon of olive oil leftover and sprinkle with salt to taste. Grill the kebabs directly over the fire on the grill grate, regularly changing so that both sides cook evenly. Cook for about 20 minutes, or until all the veggies are tender. Serve immediately with the tomato sauce on top.

26Red Lentil Sloppy Joes

Ingredients:

- Oil (1/2 tbsp.)

- Small onion, diced (1)

- Anaheim pepper, diced (1)

- Tomato paste (2 tbsp.)

- Cloves garlic, minced (3)

- Red lentils (1/2 cup)

- Water/Broth (1 1/2 cup)

- Mustard (1 tbsp.)

- Maple syrup (1 tbsp.)

- Apple cider vinegar (2 tbsp.)

- Vegan Worcestershire (1 tsp.)

- Chili powder (1 tsp.)

- Salt (1/2 tsp.)

To Serve

- 2 buns2 buns

Instructions:

1. Heat oil over medium heat in a medium pot and add the chopped onions and Anaheim pepper. Saute for 3-4 minutes, before soft, and the onions are only beginning to turn golden. Add the tomato paste and sauté for a minute. Add the garlic and cook for 1 minute.

2. To the pot, add the red lentils and 1 ½ cup of water. Bring it to a boil, and let it simmer. Cook for 10-15 minutes, stirring regularly until the lentils are pretty tender but do not fall apart.

3. Add mustard, apple cider vinegar, maple syrup, chili powder, Worcestershire, and salt. Stir to combine. Simmer until the sauce thickens a bit, for 3-5 more minutes.

4. Serve with whatever toppings and sides you love, on toasted buns!

27 Red Lentil Sloppy Joes

Ingredients:

- Oil (1/2 tbsp.)

- Small onion, diced (1)

- Anaheim pepper, diced (1)

- Tomato paste (2 tbsp.)

- Cloves garlic, minced (3)

- Red lentils (1/2 cup)

- Water/Broth (1 1/2 cup)

- Mustard (1 tbsp.)

- Maple syrup (1 tbsp.)

- Apple cider vinegar (2 tbsp.)

- Vegan Worcestershire (1 tsp.)

- Chili powder (1 tsp.)

- Salt (1/2 tsp.)

To Serve

• 2 buns2 buns

Instructions:

1. Heat oil over medium heat in a medium pot and add the chopped onions and Anaheim pepper. Saute for 3-4 minutes, before soft, and the onions are only beginning to turn golden. Add the tomato paste and sauté for a minute. Add the garlic and cook for 1 minute.

2. To the pot, add the red lentils and 1 1⁄2 cup of water. Bring it to a boil, and let it simmer. Cook for 10-15 minutes, stirring regularly until the lentils are pretty tender but do not fall apart.

3. Add mustard, apple cider vinegar, maple syrup, chili powder, Worcestershire, and salt. Stir to combine. Simmer until the sauce thickens a bit, for 3-5 more minutes.

4. Serve with whatever toppings and sides you love, on toasted buns!

28   Quinoa Chili

Ingredients:

- Uncooked quinoa (1/2 cup)

- Diced Large onion (1)

- Minced cloves garlic (6)

- Olive oil (1 tbsp.)

- 2 cups diced tomatoes (total 28 oz)

- 14oz/398 mL cup tomato sauce (1)

- Green chiles diced (1 cup) optional

- Cumin (2 tbsp.)

- Cacao powder (2 tsp.)

- Chili powder (2 1/2 tbsp.)

- Smoked paprika (1 1/2 tsp.)

- Cane sugar/any sugar (1 tsp.)

- Coriander (1/2 tsp.)

- Cayenne pepper (1/2 tsp.) OPTIONAL

- Salt & pepper

- 12 fl oz cup corn, rinsed & drained (1)

- fl oz cup kidney beans, rinsed & drained (2)

- 19 fl oz cup black beans, rinsed & drained (1)

Instructions:

Chili preparation

1. As per bag instructions, cook a half cup of quinoa and set aside.

2. Heat the olive oil over med-high heat in a wide pot. Put the onion, then cook until soft, and then add the garlic for last some seconds until the oil is hot.

3. Apply the diced tomatoes, chili powder, cooked quinoa, tomato sauce, cumin, cacao, sugar, paprika, spice, cilantro, and pepper to taste. If you find it spicy, add the Cayenne and Chiles.

4. Boil it, simmer for 30 mins.

5. Add the beans and corn and cook till heated.

6. Remove the chili from the heat and now allow it to cool.

Package

1. Uniformly spread into dehydrator trays. Dry it for 8 to 10 hrs at 145F/63C. When the beans

become dry, chili is done.

2. Pack six servings evenly in airtight packages (ziplock bags like) or vacuum seals. Store in a dry, cool & dark place.

On trail

1. Into the pot, pour the dry chili, add water (1 cup) per serving, then mix well. Just get it to a boil. Simmer for around 20 mins, stirring regularly.

Chapter 6: Dessert recipes for camping

---

1. Cracker Jack with Pretzel Treats

Ingredients

- Half stick of unsalted butter, plus a bit more for pan (3/4 cup)

- Cracker Jacks (7 cups)

- One bag of marshmallows (16-oz)

- Salted mini pretzels, chopped (4 cups)

- Kosher salt (3/4 tsp.)

- Cocktail peanuts (1 cup)

Instructions

1. Butter a 13-by-9-inch baking tray.

2. Melt butter over the moderate flame in a big Dutch oven.

3. Cook, constantly stirring, until golden brown and fragrant, for 4 to 6 minutes.

4. Retrieve from heat and stir in the marshmallow until it has melted.

5. Fold in Cracker Jackets, peanuts, pretzels and salt unless coated.

6. Move mix to the prepared skillet and push into a fine layer; cool thoroughly. Slice into 15 squares.

2. Blueberry whoopie pies

Ingredients

- All-purpose flour spooned and leveled (2 1/2 cup)

- Kosher salt (1/2 tsp.)

- Baking powder (3/4 tsp.)

- Baking soda (1/4 tsp.)

- Granulated sugar (1/2 cup)

- One stick of unsalted butter, at room temperature (1/2 cup)

- Lemon zest (1 tbsp.)

- Packed light brown sugar (1/2 cup)

- One large egg

- Mascarpone cheese (8 oz.)

- Blueberries (6 oz.)

- Lemon zest (1 tbsp.)

- Buttermilk (3 1/2 tbsp.)

- Confectioners' sugar (1/4 cup)

- Kosher salt, pinch required.

Instructions

1. Make cookies: Preheat the oven to 375 °F. Line 3 wide baking sheets with the parchment paper.

2. In a bowl, stir together flour, salt, baking powder, and baking soda.

3. Beat butter, brown sugar, granulated sugar and lemon zest with an electric mixer at normal speed until smooth and fluffy, two to three minutes.

4. Beat the egg and pour in the mixture. Beat in flour mix and buttermilk, start and finish with flour mixture, only until combined. Fold in the berries as well.

5. Scoop the batter (about 1 1/2 teaspoons each) onto the prepared baking sheets, each 2 inches

apart.

6. Bake in batches, unless puffed and the tops spring back when gently squeezed, 12 to 14 minutes.

7. Enable to cool on the baking sheets for five minutes, and then move to the wire rack to cool fully.

8. Create the filling: beat lemon zest, mascarpone, sugar, buttermilk and salt with an electric mixer at moderate speed until combined, around 1 minute.

9. Spread the filling at the bottom of half of the cookies, separating equally.

10. Sandwich with the remaining amount of the cookies.

3 Campfire Apple Pie Packets

Ingredients:

- Apple, cored and sliced (1)

- Butter (1 tbsp.)

- Brown sugar (1 1/2 tbsp.)

- Ground cinnamon (1/4 tsp.)

- Dried cranberries/Raisins (1 tbsp.) OPTIONAL

- Chopped pecans (1 tbsp.) OPTIONAL

Instructions:

1. Preheat the grill (to medium heat). Cut the nonstick foil into a 12 x 18-inch sheet.

2. Along with brown sugar, butter, and cinnamon, and dried cranberries, place the apple slices on the foil.

3. Double-fold seals securely wrap the package, allowing for a bit of space for heat expansion.

4. Place the packet on the grill, cover, and cook over medium heat for approximately 15 minutes.

5. Be careful because it would be really hot when removing it from the grill! When opening packets, use caution because when you open them, there would be hot steam.

6. Right in the packages we serve. There will be juices on the bottom of the package, so before having a bite, stir the apples gently.

4 Campfire Tarts and My First Giveaway!

Ingredients:

- Small refrigerated biscuits (1 package)
- 2 (21 oz) cup pie filling like apple, raspberry, blueberry, cherry
- Whipped cream
- Fire sticks Tarts (special equipment)

Instructions:

1. Wrap & mold one biscuit dough evenly around each tart On Fire Stick's stainless-steel cup (no greasing required).

2. Roast it over the open flame, frequently rotating till golden brown, around 1 to 2 minutes

3. From the stainless-steel cup, remove the toasted biscuit, fill with the filling of the favorite pie, and top with the whipped cream.

5 Grilled Shortcake Skewers

Ingredients:

- Strawberries
- Pineapple
- Coconut pound cake (store-bought or homemade)
- Whipped cream

Instructions:

1. Cut the fruit and the pound cake into cubes of a similar size. Thread onto BBQ skewers and grill over medium-high heat for around 6 to 8 mins, turning it again until soft is the fruit, and toasted is the pound cake. Serve it with whipped cream.

6 Berry Camping Cake

Ingredients:

- Flour (3 3/4 cups)

- Salt (1 tsp.)

- Ground cloves (1/4 tsp.)

- Ground cinnamon (1/4 tsp.)

- Ground nutmeg (1/8 tsp.)

- Ground ginger (1/8 tsp.)

- Chilled Butter, cut into tiny pieces (1 cup)

- Baking powder (1 1/2 tbsp.)

- Sugar (2 1/4 cups)

- Frozen unsweetened strawberries/other berries (50 ounces)

Instructions:

1. Pulse the flour, cinnamon, nutmeg, salt, cloves, baking powder, and ginger into a food processor. Add butter, then pulse till it is very thinly combined. To combine, add sugar, then pulse. Transfer to a resealable bag (large), and chill for about two days before ready to use.

2. Ignite forty briquets on a firepit/clean charcoal grill fire grate at the campsite and allow it to burn until it is covered with a fine ash layer. Arrange twenty coals in a 12" by using tongs. Ring; push aside the remaining coal.

3. Put in the 12-in strawberries. Dutch Footed (Camp) Oven. Spoon the mixture of flour (half) equally over the strawberries, cover the pot, and place the coals in a ring. Arrange the left ash-covered 20 coals above the Dutch oven lid in one layer.

4. Another ring is arranged of 20 new, unlit coals across the oven base and touch the heated coals (these can ignite and then have a second heat burst).

5. Cook the cake for 20 mins (don't cover the firepit or grill). Push the coals from the cover handle with tongs, remove the lid (on top, keep the coals) and spoon on the leftover flour mixture. The lid & top is replaced equally across the pot with the 2nd set of fresh coals (ash-covered).

6. Bake till golden brown is the topping & strawberry juices bubble to surface, for an extra 15-25 mins. Before eating, let it cool for 20 mins at least.

7. When using berries and not strawberries, mix with more sugar (1/4 cup) when adding them.

7 Campfire pie with cherries

Ingredients

- All-purpose flour, leveled and spooned (1 cup)

- Sugar, divided (1/2 cup)

- One stick of unsalted butter, cut into pieces (12 tbsp.)

- Toasted almonds, roughly diced (1/4 cup)

- Baking soda (1/2 tsp.)

- Traditional rolled oats, divided (1 1/2 cup)

- Two containers fresh raspberries (6-ounce)

- Kosher salt (1/2 tsp.)

Instructions

1. Preheat the oven to 375 degrees. Cover 8-inch-square baking skillet with baking paper, leaving a 1-inch overhang on all ends.

2. In a food processor, spin the flour, the butter, and 1/2 cup sugar together until a sandy texture appears, at least 10 to 12 times.

3. Shift 1/3 cup to a pot and add in 1/2 cup of oats and almonds. Squeeze to form tiny clumps; freeze.

4. In the food processor, add baking soda, salt and the leftover 1 cup of oats to the mixture. Pulse 12 to 15 times before blended.

5. Press in the bottom of the prepared skillet. Bake until lightly browned, Fourteen to 16 minutes.

6. In a bowl, mix one jar of raspberries and the remaining tablespoon of sugar. Spread all

over the pre-baked crust.

7. Spread the leftover raspberries and cooled crumb mixture on top.

8. Bake for 40 to 45 minutes till nicely browned.

9. Cool for 30 minutes in the pan, and then used the overhang to move to a wire rack to cool thoroughly.

8 Grilled Plums with Honey and Ricotta

Ingredients

- Granulated sugar (1 tbsp.)

- Ricotta (1 cup)

- Plums (6)

- Orange zest (1 tsp.)

- Shelled pistachios (1/4 cup)

- Honey (2 tbsp.)

Instructions

1. Grill heat to medium.

2. Scatter the sugar on cut sides of the plums and flame for 1 to 2 minutes, cut side down until lightly torched and start to caramelize.

3. Turn and grill, covered, for another two minutes.

4. Meanwhile, mix orange zest and ricotta in a wide bowl.

5. Move the plums to the serving plates, spoon the ricotta mix over its top, sprinkled with the honey and garnish with the pistachio.

9 Campfire cinnamon waffles roll.

Ingredients

- A packet of yeast (1/2)

- Warm milk (1/2 cup)

- Sugar (1/4 cup)

- Butter, divided (10 tbsp.)

- Salt (1/2 tsp.)

- One egg

- All-purpose flour, plus a little more for your hands (2 cups)

- Cinnamon (1 tsp.)

- Pack of light brown sugar (1/2 cup)

- Cream cheese softened (4 ounces)

- Vanilla extract (1 tsp.)

- Powdered sugar (1 cup)

- Cooking spray, Nonstick

Instructions

In the camp:

1. Punch the dough and knead it on a well-floured surface a couple of times. Roll in a thin rectangle.

2. Spread three teaspoons of softened butter over the pastry. Sprinkle of cinnamon and brown sugar.

3. Begin at one end, rolls the dough firmly into a log. Put the log seam side down on a wide chopping board or any other work surface. Slice it into six pieces.

4. Preheat the waffle iron over the campfire for several minutes.

5. When it's hot and good, spray it with a non-stick cooking spray and carefully put a roll of cinnamon inside.

6. Cover the waffle iron and heat over a bright campfire until the dough is done cooking completely; keep turning and monitoring closely.

7. Put the waffle on a plate and cover with some foil (or place it in a heated Dutch oven) to keep it warm as you cook the other waffles.

8. Spread a generous portion of icing over each cinnamon roll waffle and eat.

10 S'mores chunky pies

Ingredients

- Oil or non-stick spray for pie irons

- graham cracker squares smashed into medium crumbs (4)

- Campfire small Marshmallows (1 cup)

- chocolate chips (1/2 cup)

- cinnamon swirl bread (8 slices)

Instructions

1. Slightly spray pie iron with oil or non-stick spray.

2. Put one slice of bread in one part of the pie iron. Sprinkle with two tablespoons of chocolate chips, 1/4 of graham cracker crumbs and 1/4 cup of the Bonfire® Mini Marshmallow.

3. Put the second slice of bread on the marshmallows and cover the pie iron. Take off any leftover bread with your hands.

4. Cook the pies over the flames for two minutes, turn and cook for another minute from another side. Carefully open the pie iron and place the pie on the plate. Enjoy it!

11 Pound Cake and Berry Campfire Skillet Dessert

Ingredients

- fresh berries (12–16 oz)

- butter (1/4 cup)

- Rolo candy bars (2)

- Sugar (2 tbsp.)

- pound cake (3/4 lb)

Instructions

1. In a bowl, add the berries and the sugar and sit for 15 minutes before the juices are released.

2. Place a grill over hot coals (or use a grate). Put the butter to the 12" cast iron skillet and let it melt. Slice the cake of the pound into 1" pieces. Transfer to the warm skillet and cook until both sides are evenly toasted. Remove the pan from the flame.

3. Scatter the berries over the surface of cake cubes, and then spread the rolos on the top.

4. Wrap the skillet with foil and rest until the berries are warmed, and the chocolate melts in 5-10 minutes.

12 Campfire Chocolate Monkey Bread

Ingredients

- Pillsbury refrigerated biscuits (2 packs)

- chocolate cook (1 pack)

- pudding mix, but not instant pudding mix (1 pack)

- brown sugar (1/2cup)

- sugar (1/4cup)

- cooking spray

- butter (1/2cup)

Instructions

1. Before camping, put the brown sugar, the pudding mixture and the sugar in a big Ziploc bag.

2. At the campground, set the campfire and let it flame for at least 60 minutes to produce

hot coals.

3. Break the biscuits into pieces. Drop further into the Ziploc bag and cover it properly.

4. Melt the butter and spill over the pieces of biscuits. Close the bag and shake it again. The biscuits are expected to be very gooey.

5. Pie iron will help to dry them out, but you want them to be very well covered.

6. Spray well on all sides of the pie iron with a cooking spray. This recipe is going to fill two double size pie irons.

7. Put the biscuits over the pie iron and pour any residual mixture over the top to further coat; make sure you spare some for the final batch! You can also consider doing this halfway into cooking if you want it a little bit moister.

8. Shut the pie iron and put it in the hot coals for around 10-12 minutes, turning and spinning constantly. {We noticed that it operated well if we turned the pie iron around as well as turning it around the coals so that the front of the pie iron was not necessarily facing the same thing.

13 Dutch oven cinnamon nut splits

Ingredients

- yeast dinner rolls (12)

- brown sugar (3/4 cup)

- butter (1/3 cup)

- chopped pecans (1/2 cup)

- cinnamon (1 tbsp.)

Instructions:

1. You're going to start by having your dutch oven prepared.

2. Utilize 4-6 coals less than that of the oven's inch diameter below the bottom and four to six coals more on the top of the oven for sufficient heat in a Dutch oven.

3. Rotate the oven and lid manually at 90 degrees every 5-10 minutes while baking and detach

from the bottom heat for the last 15 minutes during baking. Cover the dutch oven with aluminum foil and non-stick cooking oil.

4. Heat rolls until it's soft. Divide the roll in two.

5. Mix brown sugar, cinnamon and nuts. Dip half of the roll in butter and roll in the cinnamon/sugar mix until it is fully covered.

6. began with a half roll and then went on in the round.

7. Then lined the same way within the circle until the bottom of the pan had been covered. Ample rolls were remaining to go on for one more loop in the second layer. Close the lid.

8. Let rise to twice the size (2-3 hours). Bake in the fire for 25-30 minutes or until the core is done.

9. Pull from the flames and go around the sides of the oven with a knife. Invert on the serving tray. Enjoy it!

11 Chocolate Lava Cake with Cherries

Ingredients

- cherry pie filling (1 can)

- lemon-lime soda (1 can)

- chocolate cake mix (1 box)

- chocolate chips (1 bag)

Instructions

1. Arrange the charcoal.

2. Apply a lining to the Dutch oven or brush with cooking oil.

3. Open the filling for the pie and pour it into the Dutch oven's bottom.

4. On top of the cherry filling, layer the chocolate cake mix.

5. Open the soda and dump over the cake mixture gently. It'll foam, so if you move slowly, it doesn't overflow.

6. Garnish the soda with the chocolate chips on top.

7. Place the cap on the Dutch oven.

8. Place 16 coals of charcoal on the oven lid.

9. Create an eight-charcoal circle that will act as the central heat for the cake to be cooked.

10. Dutch oven is placed over the circle and cooks the cake for around an hour. Depending upon the size of the Dutch oven and the warmth of the coals, it may take more or less time

11. Take away the Dutch oven from the charcoal and enjoy it.

14 Bonfire cones

Ingredients

- Waffle cones (5)

- Graham cracker pieces, crushed (1 pack)

- Chocolate chips (1 cup)

- Mini marshmallows (1 cup)

- Optional toppings:

- M &Ms, peanut butter cups, rolos, bananas, coconut, strawberries, brown sugar, nuts, butterscotch chips, anything your imagination can come up with

- Foil

Instructions

1. Coat the waffle cones with the toppings and cover with foil.

2. Keep tossing over the coals in the campfire for 5-7 minutes until it is nice and started melting.

3. They can also be placed in a 400-degree oven for 5-7 minutes. It can also be prepared in advance for a nice surprise.

15 Bourbon peach cobbler

Ingredients

- Peaches, sliced (3)

- Oil (1 tbsp.)

- Bourbon (1/2 cup)

- Granola (1 cup)

- Sugar (2 tbsp)

Instructions

1. To prepare the bourbon peach cobbler, warm the oil in a cast-iron pan and add three sliced ripe peaches.

2. After a few minutes, turn the peaches to warm on both sides, and then withdraw them from the fireplace.

3. Spill half a cup of bourbon over all the peaches and return them over the flames.

4. Add 2 tbsp of sugar and mix in the sauce until it blankets the peaches and lowers the flame by almost 5 or 10 minutes.

5. Lift the skillet from the fire and brush your peaches with a cup of granola and serve immediately.

16 S'mores with a twist

Ingredients

- Graham cracker or any chocolate chip cookies etc. (1 pack)

- Chocolate bar or any other chocolate such as Twix, Kit Kat, etc. (5 pieces)

- Marshmallows (1 pack)

Instructions

1. Take plain old s'mores and raise them to a whole new level by being inventive with your recipes.

2. Use chocolate chip cookies instead of graham crackers to create the exterior crust of your s'mores.

3. .Substitute chocolate bars with some other tasty treats such as Kit Kat, Snickers bars or peanut butter cups

17 Apple pie foil packets

Ingredients

- Apple, sliced (1)

- Brown sugar (1 ½ tbsp.)

- Unsalted butter (1 tbsp.)

- Cranberries (1 tbsp.)

- Ground cinnamon (¼ tsp.)

- Chopped nuts (1cup)

Instructions

1. A pretty balanced take on dessert, the packet of apple pie foil is like consuming pie filling.

2. Place the sliced apple, 1 tbsp of butter, 1 ½ tbsp of brown sugar, ¼ tsp of ground cinnamon, 1 tbsp of cranberries and a light sprinkling of crushed nuts on a sheet of aluminum foil.

3. Fold the aluminum foil over all of the ingredients such that all the ingredients are wrapped in a packet of the foil.

4. Put the packet on a grill over the warm fire and let it cook for around 15 minutes, then lift it from the flame and enjoy it.

18 Campfire strawberries

Ingredients

- Strawberries (1 cup)

- Marshmallow fluff (1 jar)

Instructions

1. Quick and tasty, campfire strawberries are perfect for breakfast and as a sweet dish.

2. Penetrate the surface of a strawberry with the skewer or a marshmallow poker like you do when grilling marshmallows for s'mores.

3. Dip the bottom of the strawberry in the marshmallow fluff glass jar.

4. Toast the strawberry over the flames until the fluff is light brown. Consume when it is hot.

19 Bonfire eclairs

Ingredients

- Crescent rolls (1 pack)

- Chocolate frosting for coating (1cup)

- Pre-made pudding

Instructions

1. To create this delicious cake, unroll a box of the crescent rolls to make the plain dough, tie the dough around the skewer and heat it above the campfire.

2. When the dough has golden brown, extract it from the fire to let it cool off, fill it with the pudding and coat it with the chocolate coating to make a pastry shop éclair.

20   Campfire sweet calzones

Ingredients

- ball of pizza dough (1)
- Dessert fillings of your choice (1cup)

Instructions

1. To prepare calzones, take the pizza dough and divide it in half.

2. Cover the dough with butter and then add your desired sweet toppings, such as peanut butter cups, candy bars and icing sugar, to one end of the dough.

3. When you've decided on the filling, fold the dough such that the components are on the inner side and dough crimp around the corners.

4. Put the calzone on the grill and cook until nicely browned, typically for at least 20 minutes.

21 Dessert pizza

Ingredients

- Ball of pizza dough (1)
- Dessert toppings of your choice (1 cup)
- Nutella (1 cup)

Instructions

1. Another variation on a tasty dinner, dessert pizza is better enjoyed with friends.

2. Take the pizza dough from the store and rub it with Nutella, then add on top of it your preferred sweet treats.

3. Put the dessert pizza inside a buttered cast iron pan and cook over the fireplace till the crust is nicely browned.

22 Campfire churros

Ingredients

- can of any biscuits (1)

- cinnamon sugar mix (½ cup)

- stick of butter (1)

Instructions

1. To prepare campfire churros, open a can of market bought biscuits and break them in half, then tie every biscuit around the skewer and toast them on the flame once they have finished frying.

2. Melt a stick of butter in a small bowl.

3. When the biscuits are prepared, dunk them in butter until they are thoroughly covered and then put them inside a zip lock bag loaded with the sugar and cinnamon mix (half cup of sugar and two tablespoons of cinnamon) and shake it.

4. When the churros are coated in sugar and cinnamon, it's time to celebrate them.

23 Peanut butter no-bake bars

Ingredients

- Butter (only for pan)

- Scmi-sweet baking chocolate (2 ounces)

- Peanut butter (1 cup)

- Confectioners' sugar (2 cups)

- Graham cracker crumbs (1 ½ cups)

Instructions

1. Melt the stick of butter over the campfire.

2. If the butter has been melted, retrieve from the warm fire and pour 1 cup of the peanut butter, cups powdered sugar, and 1 ½ cup of the graham cracker, crushed into crumbs,

3. Pour mixture into the 9 x 13-inch pan. Melt the 12 ounces of semi-sweet chocolate on the campfire and pour over all of the mixtures inside the pan.

4. They're ready to eat when that chocolate has chilled. This recipe is also perfect for preparing in advance to carry it to the campsite.

24 Chocolate-covered pretzels

Ingredients

- Chocolate (chips or chopped bars)
- Pretzel sticks (1 pack)

Instructions

1. For a simple and tasty cake, melt the dark or white chocolate in a skillet on the campfire.

2. Take out the pretzel sticks and dunk them in the chocolate, and coat half of the stick.

3. For a bit of a twist, throw some sprinkles or your preferred flavored candy on the chocolate when it's still hot, and then let the pretzel cool before consuming.

25 Lemon blueberry Dutch baby

Ingredients

- Pint of fresh blueberries (1)
- Juice of a lemon (1)
- Sugar (1 tsp.)
- Lemon zest (1/2 tsp.)
- Nutmeg & salt (a pinch)
- Milk (1/2 cup)
- Large eggs (2)

- All-purpose flour (1/2 cup)

Instructions

1. This campfire dessert requires a little time, but the outcomes are worth it.

2. Put 1 pint of the fresh blueberries, one lemon juice, 1teaspoon of honey, and a half teaspoon of lemon zest in either a small bowl.

3. Put aside the small bowl and stir in a large bowl, half a cup, a cup of milk, half a cup of all-purpose flour, two eggs, a pinch of the nutmeg and a bit of salt.

4. To make things simpler while camping, ingredients should be weighed at home earlier.

5. Heat the Dutch oven on the campfire, then melt the butter in it.

6. Transfer the batter mix to the Dutch oven, then cover with the lid to cook for at least thirty minutes.

7. When the cake is baked through, detach from heat and add blueberry or lemon topping. Serve and enjoy yourself.

26Coconut snowballs

Ingredients

- Shredded coconut (1 cup)

- Maple syrup (1/4 cup)

- Of almond flour (1/3 cup)

Instructions

1. Another of the easiest and tasty campfire treats, the coconut snowballs, can also be whipped together at camp in no time.

2. You need 1 cup of shredded coconut, 1/3 cup of almond flour and 1/4 cup of maple syrup.

3. Mix the ingredients in a bowl and, when blended, mold the mixture into the balls. Drop the balls in another 1/4 cup of the coconut, and enjoy eating.

27 Walnut chocolate burritos

Ingredients

- Tortillas (5)

- Walnuts, chopped (1cup)

- Chocolate chips (1 cup)

- Marshmallows (1 pack)

Instructions

1. Prepare this fast and simple campfire snack, apply the butter to the tortilla and stack it with -sweet chocolate chips, diced walnuts, small marshmallows and whatever another topping that fits your palate.

2. Roll the tortilla all over the ingredients much like you will as you fold the burrito and put the burrito over the campfire on the cast iron grill, constantly tossing till the ingredients are warm and gooey.

28 Crème lemon sandwich cookies

Ingredients

- Softened cream cheese (2 oz.)

- Lemon zest (1/2 tsp.)

- Thin lemon cookies (32)

- Confectioners' sugar (3 tbsp.)

- Lemon juice (2 tbsp.)

- Heavy cream (1/2 cup)

Instructions

1. Beat the softened cream cheese with the electric blender at moderate speed until creamy. Beat in the sugar, lemon juice and lemon zest.

2. Slowly add the cold heavy cream and beat until the peaks are stiff.

3. Sandwich the cream in 32 thin lime cookies (approximately two teaspoons per sand-wich). Make around 32 cookies.

29Cap'n Crunch Peanut Candy Bars

Ingredients

- Cap'n Crunch cereal (3 cups)

- Chopped cocktail peanuts (3/4 cup)

- Crushed pretzel sticks (1 1/2 cup)

- Creamy peanut butter (1/4 cup)

- One bag of caramel candies (11-ounce)

- Heavy cream (2 tbsp.)

- Sweet chocolate chips, melted (1 cup)

Instructions

1. Lightly oil a 9-by-9-inch baking skillet and line up with baking paper.

2. In a container, mix cereal, pretzels and peanuts. Stir caramels, peanut butter and cream in a medium saucepan, constantly stirring, until melted and fluffy, 15 to 16 mins.

3. Spillover the cereal mixture and whisk until blended.

4. Push it in the prepared pan. Chill up to the set time, around 1 hour. Slice up to 12 bars.

5. Drizzle melted chocolate on the bars. Let the bars stay till the chocolate has been set, around 1 hour.

Chapter 7: Drinks recipes for camping

1 Beach Blue Cocktail

Ingredients

- Blue Raspberry Vodka (1 1/2 oz)

- 7UP (6 oz)

- Coconut Rum (1 1/2 oz)

Instructions

1. whisk all the ingredients in a serving glass

2. Add ice as much as required

2 Pine punch cone

Ingredients

- unsweetened pineapple juice (7 1/2 ounces)

- fir or pine liqueur, e.g., Zirbenz (2 1/2 ounces)

- dark rum, such as Gosling's or Myers's (5 ounces)

- Ice

Instructions

1. In a 16-ounce container, combine the rum, pineapple juice, and liqueur

2. Seal with the tightly fitting cap

3. Cover the drink and chill till done to serve. (The mixture can be kept for at least two days.)

4. at the time of serving, shake the mix to blend properly and then spill it over ice cubes in the glass

3 Gold Rush

Ingredient

For the Gold Rush

- Bourbon (2 ounces)

- rich honey syrup (3/4 ounce)

- lemon juice (3/4 ounce)

For the rich honey syrup

- Honey (1 cup)

- Water (1/3 cup)

Instructions

For preparing Gold Rush:

1. Take a cocktail shaker filled with ice and add all the ingredients.

2. Shake it for around 15 seconds, until all are evenly combined and chilled

3. Pour it in the serving glass over a huge piece of ice

For preparing earthy honey syrup:

1. Warm the water and honey in a pan on moderate flame, constantly stirring unless all the ingredients have evenly mixed.

2. Retrieve from the flame and let it cool, then put in a fridge.

3. Keep in a tightly packed container to store; this will keep syrup fresh for almost a week

4 The Corsican Cocktail

Ingredient

- Lillet Blanc, chilled (13 ounces)

- elderflower syrup (3 1/2 ounces)

- A bottle of club soda, chilled (10-ounce)

- limoncello, chilled (7 ounces)

- fresh lemon juice (1 3/4 ounces)

- lemon twists, if desired (6)

Instructions:

- Take a large bowl or measuring pot, add limoncello, the Lillet, lemon juice and elderflower syrup in it.

- Transfer to a three-cup capacity vessel or flask using a funnel. Cover it with a tight lid and keep it in the fridge for almost eight hours

- At the time of serving, use a cocktail glass or any other glass and put 4 ounces of the stored mixture into it, then pour 1 ½ to 1 ¾ ounce of club soda over it.

- Top it with lemon wedges if wanted, and then serve.

- On the other hand, put the entire ingredients in a five cup punch vessel and instantly serve.

5 Rob Roy in the Flask

Ingredients:

- blended scotch (5 oz)

- Water (1 1/2 oz)

- dashes of Angostura bitters (5)

- sweet vermouth (1 1/2 oz)

Instructions:

- Put all the ingredients in a serving glass and whisk it without adding ice

- Pour the cocktail into the flask and cover it

- Either pour it over some pieces of ice or sip it directly from the flask and enjoy

6 Campfire Margaritas

Ingredients

- A can of tequila + some more splashes (12 ounces)

- Three cans of water (12 ounces)

- one can of triple sec (6 ounces)

- A can of limeade (12 ounces)

- margarita salt (a pinch)

- Fresh limes, each sliced into six wedges (2)

Instructions

1. It is a convenient way to use a limeade can for measuring the ingredients used in the recipe.

2. Put all the ingredients in the zip lock bag and double bag it to keep it secure during traveling.

3. The zip lock bag should be freeze for a few days before taking it to the camp. Keep it in an ice chest while traveling.

4. At the time of serving, smash the baggie mixture till it gets slushy.

5. Use eight cocktail glasses and cover the rim by dipping in the salt. Also, rub a lemon slice over the rim. After that, pour the slush into the glasses and garnish with lemon wedges.

7 Campfire s'mores Hot Chocolate Cocktail

Ingredients

- Milk (1 cup)

- heavy cream (1 cup)

- chocolate chips, semi-sweet (1/2 cup)

- graham cracker, crushed (1)

- jar/ Pack of marshmallows fluff or marshmallow (1)

- honey (2 tbsp)

- chocolate syrup (1/4 cup)

- simple syrup (1 tbsp)

- chocolate pudding mix powder (1/4 cup)

- whiskey (2 oz.)

Instructions

1. Take a pan and add heavy cream and milk to it, then cook over moderate heat.

2. Meanwhile, melt the chocolate chips in the oven by placing them in a small bowl and heating for 30 seconds.

3. First, dip the glasses' rim in the melted chocolate and then dip them in the chunky graham cracker and put them aside.

4. Pour remaining melted chocolate into the cream and milk, and then add simple syrup, chocolate syrup and honey and stir together. Add in the pudding mixture gradually and keep folding until it blends properly. Heat the mixture to low flame and then withdraw from flame.

5. Whisk the mixture in the whiskey and then pour it into all the prepared glasses. Garnish with the marshmallow fluff or mini marshmallow and toast the marshmallows using any torch. It's ready to be served.

8 Marshmallow Easy Syrup with Rye Whiskey

Ingredients

- Sugar (1 cup)

- Bulleit Rye whiskey (6 oz.)

- Marshmallows (8-10)

- Water (1 cup)

- Splash single malt whisky (1)

Instructions

1. Take a saucepan and add water and sugar to it. Heat until sugar dissolves. Add marshmallows to the saucepan and heat at the higher flame for about five minutes, and keep stirring until they are melted.

2. Now strain the marshmallow's simple syrup in an airtight jar or bottle and waste the remaining solid marshmallows. Put it aside to chill. The syrup can be stored for at least two weeks in the fridge.

3. Take a champagne glass and add Laphroaig and Bulleit to it. Pour in around two oz of simple syrup in the glass, or more can be added according to the taste. Put some ice and garnish with torched marshmallows. Enjoy

9 Campfire exotics

Ingredients

- Dry red wine (2 ounces)

- Ice (1 bowl)

- Lemon-lime soda (2 ounces)

- Lemon slice, for topping (5)

Instructions

1. Take a cocktail glass or cocktail shaker and add the soda and wine to it.

2. Shake or stir it well and pour it in the glass over the ice cubes

3. Garnish the drink with lemon wedges and enjoy

10 Mexican Chilled Mocha

Ingredients

- Unsweetened cocoa powder (3 tablespoons)

- Dry milk powder (2 tablespoons)

- Instant coffee creamer (1 tablespoon)

- Sugar (2 tablespoons)

- Cinnamon (¼ teaspoon)

- Cayenne (¼ teaspoon)

- A pinch of salt

- Instant coffee (1 packet)

Instructions

1. Take a mug and add all the dry ingredients to its bottom.

2. Put two tbsp of warm water and mix until a paste is formed.

3. Keep adding the rest of the water slowly and constantly stir.

4. Coffee is ready to indulge.

11 Rocket Flame

Ingredients

- Hot cocoa mix (1 packet)

- Hot water (8 ounces)

- Cliff shot energy gel double espresso (1)

- A spoonful of instant coffee

Instructions

1. Take a coffee mug or any mug of choice, add all the ingredients mentioned above.

2. Stir and it's ready to be served. Take a sip and enjoy

12 NUUN Drink

Ingredients

- One Nuun tablet (try the orange flavor or citrus fruit)

- Black tea (1 bag)

- Hot water (16 ounces)

Instructions

1. Place your tea in warm water in a mug.

2. Add the tablet to it and stir to dissolve.

3. The tea is ready

13 Creamy Orange Power Shake

Ingredients

- Tang (1 packet)

- Vanilla extracts (1-2 drops)

- Vanilla protein powder, check the jar as serving sizes may differ (1)

- Coldwater (12 ounces)

Instructions

1. Take a water bottle, or if the shaker style bottle is available, it will be great.

2. Add the dry ingredients to the bottle.

3. Add on the vanilla and then pour water into the bottle. Shake it well.

4. Better the shaking, the frostier it will be. The milkshake is ready to enjoy

14 NUUN Berry Camp Fizz

Ingredients

- Lemon + lime NUUN tablet (1)
- Tri-berry NUUN tablet (1/2)
- Water (8 ounces)
- Tequila (1.5 ounces)

Instructions

1. Do chill the tequila and water before using it.
2. Add the NUUN tablets into the mug. Pour water in it and spill some tequila over it. Mix it well so that the tablets are completely dissolved. The fizz is ready to be served.

15 Snow conoid Julep

- Rye whiskey (2 ounces)
- Mint leaves (4-5)
- Simple syrup (1/2 ounces)
- Fresh snow, as needed.

Instructions

1. Add some mint leaves after bruising them a little in the 8-ounce cup.
2. Place some fresh snow in the cup. Garnish with simple syrup or rye and stir the drink well. It's ready to be served.

16 Mulled cider

Ingredients

1. Stick of cinnamon (1)
2. cardamom pods (1-2)

3. Piece of ginger (1-2 inch)

4. star of anise pod (1)

5. cloves (1-2)

6. allspice berries (2)

Instructions

1. Take a saucepan and add all the whole spices along with the apple cider and put some orange wedges in it. Simmer it for around 15 minutes.

2. Pour it in the mugs. If desired, some brandy or any other alcoholic beverage can also be added to it. Cider is ready, enjoy

17 Virginjack

Ingredients

- granulated sugar (1 ½ cups)

- water (1 ½ cups)

- fresh-squeezed lime juice (1)

Instructions

1. Add all the ingredients to the saucepan and boil over moderate heat; keep constantly stirring unless the sugar is dissolved. Remove it from the flame and let it cool.

2. For serving, add one teaspoon of this mixture to the ginger beer glass and serve with fresh cut lemon slices.

3. It can be stored for more than a week in the refrigerator.

18 Golden milk

Ingredients

- almond milk (1 cup)

- piece of thinly sliced, unpeeled turmeric, or turmeric powder (1 one-inch/1/2 teaspoon)

- virgin coconut oil (1)

- whole black peppercorns (¼ tsp)

- piece of thin-sliced, unpeeled ginger (1 half-inch)

- water (1 cup)

- honey (1 tsp)

- Ground cinnamon (1/2 tsp)

Instructions

1. Take a saucepan and add all the ingredients except for the cinnamon; heat it until boils. Then reduce the heat to simmer for 10 minutes.

2. It can be stored in a tight lid container for almost five days, and when you need to use, just heat it over a campfire and drink.

3. It can be served instantly by straining through a sieve. Top it with the ground cinnamon while serving

19Strawberry Lemonade

Ingredients

- Granulated sugar (1 cup)

- Water, divided (6 cups)

- Strawberries, sliced in half (1 lb.)

- Freshly squeezed lemon juice, from about ten lemons (1 cup)

- Ice

- Mint leaves, if desired

Instructions

1. Take a medium pan and add a cup of water and sugar. Heat over medium flame and stir until the sugar is fully dissolved. Let the mixture cool.

2. Add strawberries and a cup of water in a blender. Keep blending until the puree is formed.

Use a fine sieve, and strain the strawberries puree, waste the solid left on the sieve.

3. Take a pitcher and add strawberry puree, simple syrup, 4 cups of water and lemon juice to it.

4. More water can be used to adjust the taste.

5. For serving, use ice and mint as per taste.

20   Whisked Strawberry Milk

Ingredients

- Heavy cream (1/4 cup)

- Milk

- Strawberry milk powder (1 tbsp)

- Ice

Instructions

1. Take a medium bowl and add the strawberry milk and cream to it. Beat until the peaks formed are stiff.

2. Take a large neck glass and fill it with ice. Pour milk to fill ¾ of the glass, then scoop whipped mixture of strawberry over the milk. The milk is ready to serve. Enjoy

21 Virgin basil cranberry sangria

Ingredients

- Cranberry juice (3 cups)

- A can of seltzer (12-oz.)

- Frozen cranberries (1/3 cup)

- Sliced orange (1)

- Apple, sliced and cored (1)

- Packed basil leaves (1/4 cup)

- Juice of one orange (1/2 cup)

- Ice

Instructions

1. Add the cranberry juice, seltzer and orange juice in a wide pitcher. Put the basil and fruits and whisk to blend.

2. At the time of serving, pour it over ice and enjoy

22 Virgin piña colada

Ingredients

- A bag of frozen pineapple pieces (10-oz.)

- Large scoops of ice cream (about 1 cup)

- Coconut milk (1 cup)

- Pineapple juice (1/2 cup)

- Pineapple slices, for garnish.

- Maraschino cherry, for garnish.

Instructions

1. Add ice cream, pineapple juice, frozen pineapples and coconut milk in a large blender and blend it well.

2. Pour into the serving glasses and top with the maraschino cherry and pineapple slices.

23 Flawless Shirley Temple

Ingredients

- Lemon-lime soda (3 cups)

- Grenadine (4 tsp)

- Ice

- Maraschino cherries, for garnish

- Juice of a lime (1)

Instructions

1. Add ice in four serving glasses.

2. Pour lime juice in each glass, then add soda to it equally.

3. Garnish with grenadine

4. Serve it along with maraschino cherry

24 Perfect arnold pint

Ingredients

For the lemonade

- Water, divided (3 cups)

- Juice of six large lemons (3/4 cup)

- Granulated sugar (3/4 cup)

For the tea

- Water (4 cups)

- Black tea bags (5)

- Lemon wedges, for garnish

- Ice

- Honey (1/3 cup)

- Fresh mint, for garnish

Instructions

Lemonade preparation

1. Add sugar and 1 cup of water to a medium pot and heat it over a moderate flame. Keep

stirring to dissolve the sugar and let it simmer for two more minutes. Now remove from the heat and let it cool.

2. Now pour the remaining two cups of water, simple syrup and lemon juice. The lemonade is ready.

Tea preparation

1. Take water in a medium saucepan and boil it over medium flame. Put some honey in the pan and whisk to dissolve.

2. Now remove from the heat and add the tea bags to the saucepan. Let the bag stay in for 5 minutes. Cool it at room temperature.

3. Pour this tea and lemonade together in a wide pitcher and stir. Serve in glasses and garnish with lemon slices and mints.

25 Glow Water

Ingredients

- Cans of seltzer water (3)

Cucumber mint:

- Cucumber, cut into 1/2" rounds (1)

- Lemon, thinly sliced (1)

- Sprigs mint (1)

Peach ginger:

- Sliced peach (1)

- Cinnamon stick (1)

- Ginger, skin peeled and sliced into spheres (1)

Strawberry lime:

Ingredients

- Strawberries, sliced in halves (2)

- Lime, finely sliced (1)

Instructions

1. Pour the seltzer water into the glass and add the ingredients of choice. Mix it well to release the flavor from the ingredients.

2. It can be served instantly or can be chilled in the fridge before ready to drink.

26 Frosted Lemonade

Ingredients

- Freshly squeezed lemon juice (1/2 cup)

- Sugar (1/2 cup)

- Water (2 cups)

- Vanilla ice cream (6 cups)

- Sliced lemons, for garnish

Instructions

1. Take a pitcher and mix sugar and lemon juice in it. Whisk until sugar is properly dissolved. Add some water to dilute it.

2. Then put lemonade and ice cream in the blender and blend until consistency is smooth. Distribute the blend in four cups and garnish with lemon wedges before serving.

27 Rum lemonade punch

Ingredients

- Lemonade (4 oz.)

- Coconut rum (2 oz.)

- Pineapple juice (2 oz.)

- Dark rum (1 oz.)

Instructions

1. Take a wide serving glass, fill it with ice cubes, and then add coconut rum, lemonade, and pineapple juice.

2. Stir it gently with a spoon. A cocktail shaker can also be used to blend the ingredients.

3. Pour it in the glass and add some dark rum over it; it will start floating on the top and slowly merge into the drink, giving an ombre appearance. It is ready to serve

28 Mermaid Lemon drinks:

Ingredients

- Blue curaçao (1/4 cup)

- Ice (2 cups)

- White rum (1 cup)

- Lemon slices (4)

- Lemonade (2 cups)

- Maraschino cherries (8)

Instructions

1. Fill the glass with ¼ cup of ice and add ¼ cup of rum and a small quantity of blue curacao to it. The ice will give the ombre effect.

2. Then pour this liquid over the ½ cup of lemonade.

3. Use an umbrella or toothpick with skewed maraschino cherries or lemon slice and top it on the drink when ready to be served.

29 Popsicle lemon Punch

Ingredients

- Lemon-lime soda (4 cups)

- A can of seltzer (12-oz.)

- Strawberry Fruit Pops Popsicle (3)

- Cut strawberries, some more for topping (1 cup)

- Lemonade (4 cups)

- Mangoes, cut in cubes, some more for topping (2)

- Mango Fruit Pops Popsicle (3)

Instructions

1. Take a wide pitcher and strawberries, seltzer, soda, mangoes and lemonade to it. Stir well and pour in the serving glasses.

2. Garnish the drink with mango and strawberry chunks.

3. A Popsicle can also be used as a topping.

30 Purple Berry Punch

Ingredients

- Five mint leaves, some more to garnish

- Lemon wheels, some more to garnish (3)

- Ice (for serving)

- Six blueberries, plus more for garnish

- A can of Red Bull Purple Sugar-free Edition

- Fresh lemonade

Instructions

1. Take a glass and add lemon wheels, mints and blueberries.

2. Put some ice in the glass and add only one part of the fresh lemonade and four parts of the Red Bull Sugar-free Purple Edition.

3. Stir all the ingredients well. Top with some more blueberries, lemon wheels and mint leaves. Enjoy

31 Lime zinger

Ingredients

- Cucumber cut into strips (2)

- Lime wheels (3)

- Ice

- Red bull lime sugar-free edition

- White grape juice (1 cup)

- Strawberries, sliced in halves (1 cup)

Instructions

1. Take a glass and add ice, lemon wheels and cucumber to it. Pour 8 ounces of Red Bull Lime Sugar-free edition in the glass.

2. Then add 2 ounces of white grapes juice. Stir well and top it with the sliced strawberries. It's ready to be served.

32 Watermelon Bellini

Ingredients

- Watermelon cut into cubes (1 cup)

- sparkling cider or Champagne (1 cup)

Instructions

1. Use a blender to make watermelon puree.

2. Take four cocktail glasses and evenly add the puree to all of them.

3. Pour the sparkling cider or the champagne over it. A piece of watermelon can be used as a topping.

33 Sparkling Honey Lemon squash

Ingredients

- Sparkling water or club soda, cooled (1 liter)

- Coldwater (1/2 cup)

- Honey, should be lightly colored) (1/2 cup)

- Ice

- Granulated sugar (1/2 cup)

- Fresh lime juice (1 cup)

- Fresh mint, for garnish

Instructions

1. Take a pitcher and add sugar and ½ cup water to it. Stir is vigorous until the sugar is completely dissolved.

2. Add honey and whisk till it blends well.

3. Pour in some lime juice and stir. Then add sparkling water or club soda and stir again. Add mint leaves and ice before serving

34 Raspberry Sherbet Party Punch

Ingredients

Raspberry Punch Ingredients:

- Bottle of Sierra Mist Sprite or 7-up cooled (2 Liter)

- Raspberry Sherbet Ice cream or any flavor of choice (6-8 scoops)

- A can of Fruit punch or pink lemonade (12oz)

- Bottle Club Soda chilled (2 Liter)

- A can of Pineapple juice, melted in the refrigerator (12oz)

For garnish (it is optional)

- For garnish, frozen or fresh raspberries

- For garnish, fresh or canned pineapple slices

Instructions

1. Pre-scoop the ice cream and place it on a plastic wrap-lined baking dish. Just before serving, freeze and add ice cream so it stays frozen in the punch.

2. Combine two cans of juice in the punch bowl. Pour Club Soda and Sierra Mist in and stir until mixed.

3. If needed, add slices of pineapple and raspberries and garnish with the scooped sherbet when ready to serve.

4. It will remain chilled due to the ice cream.

Conclusion

Regardless of the time, present-day life will cause you to feel run-down, desolate, and separated from the ones you love. The outdoors is the best spot to fix your ills, increment your spirit, and lift your connections. It is a simple fix, it appears.

For a few, outdoors is an alarming and bold experience. Taking risks, going outside, and investigating the natural life is, without a doubt, a learning opportunity. For quite a long while, the outdoors has been a serene encounter.

Generally speaking, as you set up the entirety of your future excursions, we trust this book will be a genuine ally for you and can lead you to have the inventive transformations that empower you to make food a cheerful and exceptional piece of the undertakings from this point forward.

Printed in Great Britain
by Amazon